Imam Muhammad Shirazi

The

Family

Translated by Ali Adam

fountain books

BM Box 8545
London WC1N 3XX
UK
www.fountainbooks.co.uk

Associated publisher:
Al-Kawthar Fountain Books
PO Box 11851
Dasmah
35159
Kuwait

First published 1999

© *fountain books*

British Library Cataloguing in Publication Data.

A catalogue record for this book is available from the British Library.

ISBN   1-903323-00-2

Distributor:
Alif International, 109 Kings Avenue, Watford, Herts. WD1 7SB, UK. Telephone: + 44 1923 240 844, Fax: +44 1923 237 722

In the Name of Allah, The Beneficent The Merciful.
All Praise is to Him, Lord of the Worlds.
Let Allah's Blessings be upon Muhammad
and upon his righteous and pure family,
and His curse be upon all those who are their enemies.

Table of Contents

vi

Translator's Foreword

Family life and related issues such as marriage, divorce, parenthood, underage pregnancy and abortion are areas of great discussion and dispute in the 'western' world today. The facts emanating from various societies in the 'developed' world show that the current state of affairs is unsustainable and illogical and will inevitably result in the decline and self-destruction of these societies. A prime and oft-quoted[1] example of this is Italy where, being a Catholic country, one would expect the birth rate to be high. However with a reproduction rate of only 1.3 children per couple it is clear that the population is not being sustained or replaced and is dwindling. It requires a live reproduction rate of at least 2.0 children per couple to maintain population levels each generation. This story is repeated throughout the European Union where the Republic of Ireland despite also experiencing a sharp drop in the 'fertility' rate is the only country where rates are at 'generation replacement level'.[2] At these rates, Italy's abortion statistics at around 150,000 per year[3] seem an unaffordable luxury as they do in the other countries of the EU. The use of the term 'fertility rate' according to these statistics also appears to be a little disingenuous, as it does not take into account the number of terminations each year. The number of live births per woman is not a valid reflection of true fertility, because a conception subsequently terminated can also be regarded as a statistic of fertility.

The killing of children is deemed wrong in the Qur'an and hence in Islam:

' *And kill not your children for fear of want, We will sustain them and you. Indeed, the killing of your children is a great sin.*'[4]

In many places in the Qur'an also, evidence is brought that previous nations and generations were brought down by their sinning:

'*Do they not travel through the earth and see what was the End of those before them? They were even superior to them in strength and in the traces (they have left) in the land: but Allah did call them to account for their sins, and none had they to defend them against Allah.*[5]

ix

Hence we can see that the concept of sin is not just an abstraction with no relevance or effect in the real world but it is a way to the downfall of human society.

One man who has witnessed such a downfall in his own beloved society is Grand Ayatollah Imam Muhammad Shirazi, a prolific religious scholar and authority now living in Iran. In his book *Our Life of Half a Century Ago* written in Arabic and yet to be translated, he describes the ease, simplicity and purity of Islamic life in 'Iraq – particularly the cities of Najaf and Karbala – 50 years ago. He then tells of a gradual decline and erosion of basic Islamic tenets on a societal level and the adoption of eastern and western secularisation. This experience has lead to the main theme which runs through virtually all of Imam Shirazi's books namely a call for the gradual reinstitution of Islamic tenets, laws, principles, and commandments in all areas of life – legal, economic, political, social, and spiritual.

The Family in Islam is one such book of Imam Shirazi's. In it he highlights the problems he sees primarily in Islamic societies today from the phenomenon of unmarried young men and women through to birth control and contraception. He calls for a return to the simplicity he experienced in his youth and draws our attention to the Islamic teachings and laws in this vital area of life. As well as being a call to the Muslim world to revert to the true teachings of the Qur'an and the Prophet and Imams, this book can also be of use as an introduction to others who seek some answers to the social problems of today. Islam has detailed teachings, which promise success in every area of human life on individual and societal levels, and what's more their practicality has been historically proven despite being under constant attack from the outset until the present day. It was not so long ago that Islam was berated for allowing divorce, which is religiously permitted and spoken about in great detail in the Qur'an, yet now it has been adopted by the very societies that formerly forbade it. However picking and choosing Islamic teachings to suit fashion or whims is not the key to success. Rather the key to success is to implement the Islamic ideology in all areas of life by following God's guidance for mankind.

'*They follow guidance from their Lord and they are the ones who will prosper.*'[6]

Publisher's Foreword

The family is the very core of society. As it declines so falls society. As it ascends so ascends society.

From this precept, comes the importance placed by the divine religions upon the family, as well as the importance placed by deviant philosophies on the notion of the non-essentiality of the family, because the disappearance of the family means the disappearance of a virtuous society.

To destroy is easier than to build. The pickaxes of Freemasonry, Marxism, Existentialism, Sartreism, and Nihilistic philosophies have swung into action to reduce the edifice of human society to rubble. Through this demolition they have reaped great returns, and have achieved a victory over high morals, and have succeeded in driving European man towards perdition. These destructive elements have now arrived in Islamic societies, spreading instability and disintegration aimed at destroying the family structure whereas Islam stands in direct opposition to these ideologies. For Islam strives to provide a firm support for the family, to build a family, which is stable, calm and has a goal and direction. This is what every human being looking for happiness in life is searching for, and it cannot be achieved save through early marriage and through a close relationship with the partner and the children in an atmosphere of virtue, faith, truth, and self sacrifice. This can only be realised through simplicity and by the casting off of obsolete fetters and false traditions, for the pure family begets a pure generation, an upright generation, a generation which carries the community forward to progress and fruition.

This is the basis of Imam Shirazi's valuable effort in which he puts forward ideas and solutions to the problems of society. He deals with human society in its widest sense and studies contemporary topics such as the growth of the family and discusses views promoting the limiting of offspring and explains the Islamic position regarding this notion and other related ideas. Furthermore, he tackles certain modern problems faced by the principle of marriage and offers solutions to these problems, proposing a social programme to solve this once and for all in so far as the phenomenon of celibacy will disappear from Islamic societies.

Despite the brevity of this book, it contains important ideas coming from a man well known in Islamic circles as a source of religious knowledge and for his important services to society and as the contributor of hundreds of books to the library of Islam. His ideas are important because they spring from an understanding of history and from long experience in the field of social work. He does not propound the religious view alone but marries it with historical understanding and practical experience.

Author's Introduction

'The family in Islam' is the name of this short book, which I have written as a basic guide to an important aspect of life, which the laws of the West in Islamic countries have worked at destroying and continue to do so. I have witnessed from beginning to end a half-century of family matters and what I see latterly bears little or no resemblance to what I saw formerly. With the adoption by Muslims of Western laws, both their religion and their worldly life have disappeared, as Allah says in His book the Qur'an: *'They lose both this world and the next: That is indeed the manifest loss.'*[1]

Many Muslims, and not least their governments, have welcomed the West and lapped up its laws thinking that this was a path to liberation from the tyranny of the Ottoman and Qajar empires whose flawed Islam and complete isolation after the fall of their governments towards the West have been witnessed. They bring to mind the words of the poet:

'He who seeks refuge in 'Amr on being tortured is like one seeking refuge in fire from the burning sun'.

Or the words of another:

'I complained about 'Amr and when I left him and found other neighbours I wept for 'Amr'.

There is no doubt that the Ottoman and Qajar empires acted out with the range of Islam and for this reason, the countries of Islam fell under the control of the West and the East. But there is also no doubt that the parable for Muslims in this respect became the example of the Ummayads and the Abbasids, as the poet also says:

'Ah would that the tyranny of the sons of Marwan[2] return to us,

And would that the justice of the sons of 'Abbas[3] never was'.

Muslims had thus become an embodiment of one who has 'forgotten both the paths'. For they were, under the Ummayads and the 'Abbasids, diminished in matters of religion and of earthly life, but under the auspices of the West and the East, they were, except in a very few circumstances, completely bereft of both spheres. Allah alone knows how much we can bear of oppression and repression and deviation from His laws until the correct Islamic situation returns to us. However, we should realise that this return is not possible without

1

awareness. By awareness we mean awareness of the laws of Islam, from the notion of 'a single community without geographical borders', through to fraternity whereby every Muslim in any province of Islam is treated in all his affairs as if he is from that province, and freedom, whereby every thing is free except that which is prescribed as illegal, through to all the other vital Islamic laws so profusive in number.

Each law in Islam is a vital entity promoting life, as the Qur'anic verse says: '*Respond to Allah and His messenger when He calls you to that which will enliven you*'.[4]

This awareness, however, will only occur when Muslims have come together in organisations and political parties and groups whereby they will be in a state of utmost realism and direction, integrity and moral rectitude. Thus Allah may surround Muslims with His kindness and salvage them from this abyss the like of which they have not fallen into from the first light of Islam until this century. This is because Allah only conducts affairs by providing the ways and means to them. As He says in His book in the story of 'Dhu Al-Qarnain[5]', repeatedly: '*Then he followed a way*'[6], or as happened to the people of Israel when they went against His commands, He made them wander in the wilderness for forty years.

The aforesaid requires continuous effort and enduring patience. Do we not see that the *Khums* tax, given its importance, is only mentioned in the Qur'an once[7], while the word 'perseverance' and its derivatives are mentioned seventy times. In the *hadith* or tradition of the prophet it is said: "*As a part of faith, patience has the station of the head in relation to the body. Just as there is no good in a body without a head, there is no good in a faith that is not accompanied by patience*".

If then we work towards this and call upon Allah night and day, then it is hoped that the greatness of Muslims will be returned to them along with their independence and autonomy. Allah alone grants success and is the sole refuge.

The Holy City of Qum
Muhammad Shirazi
8th Jamadi-II, 1415 Hijra. (1995)

Section One

The Law of Matrimony

In Creation, In Civilisations and In Religions

God[8] has said in his masterful book: *'And of everything we have created pairs so that you might take notice'*.[9] The law of pairs is so deeply intrinsic to created objects that one does not find any atom or galaxy or anything smaller or larger than these that is not subject to this law. If one looks to creation in all its vastness and what it holds, from stars and planets, air and water, trees and rocks, to animals and humans, one cannot but concede as to the integrated perfection of this system in so far as each one complements and perfects the other. Each proceeds according a precise and balanced system which is only violated and traversed by humankind who were given by God the responsibility of administering themselves after having been sent messengers and having had the limits of behaviour laid out and the laws made clear. Mankind then took up this responsibility but did not carry it out, as it should be - excepting God's faithful servants - at times falling into oppressiveness, at other times into ignorance. In the Qur'an Allah states: *'We did indeed offer trusteeship to the heavens and the earth and the mountains but they refused to take it being afraid thereof. But man undertook it, though he is unjust and ignorant'.*[10]

If one leafs through the pages of human history, over and above the instructions of religion, one realises that the family system, procreation, the avoidance of inbreeding, the avoidance of marital infidelity, instability and abuse are matters of human nature and psyche (*'The fitra (intrinsic nature) of Allah upon which He has created the people.'*[11]). Even amongst primitives and pagans and those who did not observe any law, from time to time their inherent nature would shudder and would manifest itself in some form of law or in the form of customs and traditions. It is no delusion that we turn to custom and tradition to prove this, nor indeed to divine law which corresponds to inherent human nature, for all that the divine law rules necessary so does the intellect, and vice versa. The concordance and mutual agreement of humanity over a certain matter, despite their

3

diverse nations, civilisations and religions, points to the deep-rootedness of that matter in the human psyche. In this section, we will review in brief the findings of naturalists and anthropologists as well as the religious view in this field.

The Law of Matrimony in Creation

This vast creation from the smallest atom to the largest galaxy comprises of tribes and peoples based upon the system of pairs. Every element is formed from atoms, and every atom is composed of negative electron and positive proton. The occurrence of any imbalance in the ratios and equilibrium of these charges will result in the instability of the atom, and the atom will then try to return to a stable state by discharging a formidable energy known as atomic energy. Likewise in creation there are two complementing forces - magnetism and electricity - neither of which can exist without the other. Then magnetism is composed of two polarities - north and south - and electricity of two charges - positive and negative - according to scientists.

In the Vegetable World

Allah has said in the Qur'an: '*All praise to He who has created all the pairs, of which grow in the earth, and of yourselves, and of that which you have no knowledge.*'[12] Every plant contains a masculine and feminine member, which upon their maturity pollination occurs and then fruition. Granted there are types of plants and trees which do not need this depth and complexity but they are like humans who have two independent members, which co-operate mutually in order to produce fruition, as is the case with the palm tree and papaya tree and others.

In the Animal World

Animals whether quadrupeds, bipeds or reptiles, amphibians, fish or birds, are subject to the law of pairs. He (Allah) has said: '*Originator of the heavens and the earth has made out of yourselves pairs and of the beasts pairs . . .*'[13] So they strive, because of the forces placed

4

within them, to procreate and multiply and to preserve their species. Mothers extend affection to their offspring after birth or hatching and prepare the appropriate environment for their growth and development and defend them with their lives against the dangers, which surround them.

The Law of Pairs in Human Civilisations

There is no doubt that there are differences between humans and other creatures. Humans have a certain freedom of choice and will whereas animals are driven and determined. There is also no doubt that there is a difference among peoples with regards to systems and laws to an extent, which at times is contradictory and incompatible. However it is not right that we take this difference as being the most fitting expression of the matrimonial system. Indeed, this synopsis does not hold true for all areas of the nature of the family, so we will concern ourselves to the areas upon which peoples have been in agreement from the earliest times as civilisations and peoples. This will no doubt fulfil our purpose. Particularly regarding marriage and childbearing, libertinism, and the system of rights.

In the following pages, we will deal with matrimonial laws from the earliest times until the present day.

1. The Civilisation of the Valley of the Euphrates and the Tigris (Mesopotamia)

Matrimony was deemed to be greatly important in the Sumerian civilisation where they promoted marriage and repudiated celibacy. Marital infidelity was regarded by them as a crime punishable in detailed laws by death. The two adulterers if there were witnesses to the crime would be bound and thrown into water to drown, and if there were no witnesses then the woman could exonerate herself by an oath.

Amongst the Assyrians, the matter was much the same where marital fidelity was compulsory and infidelity was punishable either by death to both parties by drowning, or by them being whipped, or by their

5

hair being torn out, or by the amputation of the ears.

The Assyrians also called for a high birth rate in moral laws in which they considered abortion a serious crime punishable by execution. They considered a beating, which led to abortion as a crime punishable by fifty lashes, forced labour and in some cases execution.

The Babylonians specified more than sixty rules regarding the preservation of the family and stressed the seriousness of adultery and the implementation of punishment by drowning for the perpetrator.[14]

2. Ancient Egyptian Civilisation

Ancient Egyptian texts afforded marriage a high importance. Adultery was forbidden and its perpetrator was threatened with the most violent punishments, according to historians. The unfaithful husband would be subjected to flogging and the unfaithful wife would be subjected to the amputation of the nose. Adultery was one of the pretexts for divorce among them without distinction between the man and the woman.

In the civilisation of Osiris, dead persons used to bear with them to their graves a document testifying to their probity and fidelity in order to obtain mercy in the afterlife.

3. European Civilisations

In Sparta, celibacy was a crime in which the bachelor forfeited the right to vote and to watch public spectacles and so on.

In Rome, celibacy was forbidden and considered a state in contravention of their religion punishable by beating or flogging with regard to the age of the individual [15], and by increasing taxes and forbidding them from inheritance unless they married within 100 days of the death of the legator.[16]

They regarded adultery as a grave offence punishable by death or by banishment from the country for life.

The punishment for one who caused the abortion of a pregnant woman was banishment or the confiscation of his property.

They laid down the so called Julian[17] law specifically for marriage aimed at making marriage common and calling for a high birth rate and a reduction in taxes in relation to the number of offspring up to the number of three children, when taxes would be lifted completely just as bonds would be lifted from any woman who had given birth to three children.

Constantine made adultery punishable by death, and any such dishonour during the age of Augustinian was punishable by execution or confiscation of possessions.

4. The Civilisation of the American Continent

In the Aztec civilisation, in Central America adultery was a sin whose punishment was death by strangulation and then stoning without distinction between man and woman.

In the civilisation of the Incas in the Andes, marriage was compulsory and celibacy was forbidden and there used to be an observer from the Incas who would roam the villages and the countryside to make sure that celibates would marry.

5. The Civilisation of Ancient Japan

In Ancient Japan, women were known for marital fidelity or faced death. If a husband came upon his wife *in flagrante delicto*, it was his right to kill her and her lover on the spot. Certain of their leaders have added that if a husband has killed his wife in these circumstances and let the other man go free then he himself deserves the punishment of death.

Even the sect of the Samurai who insisted upon remaining without marrying until the age of thirty made it incumbent upon themselves to marry and produce at least two children.

Chastity was a great virtue among the Japanese so that some women would even kill themselves when their virtue was exposed to danger.

6. Among Pre-Islamic Arabs

The Arabs concerned themselves with lineage and descent, and this interest drove them to such depths and precision in the organisation of the family and the tribes and peoples that it became to them an art and a science.[18]

They used to encourage early marriage beginning with age sixteen for men and twelve or less for girls so if a girl reached eighteen or twenty without marriage, she would be viewed with concern.

The veil was widespread in the various Arab lands in many forms just as the custom of circumcision was widespread even for girls.
They used to forbid marriage to close relatives and fornication was regarded as a sin, which if they were able to punish it, did so with severe punishments.[19] In certain circumstances, the adulteress would be separated and isolated in the house and would remain in this way un-married until death.

Marital Relationships in the Major Religions

Allah says in the Qur'an in prohibition of adultery: '*Verily it is a vulgarity and a vileness and an evil path to follow*'.[20]
The use of the expression vulgarity, together with the particular past tense verb in Arabic (*Kaana*) gives the command an eternal and static quality with reference to God's abstraction from time and the singularity of his law in creation, a notion which is not confined solely to Islam but is present in the remainder of the religions, because religion is one in the realm of God, just as the inherent nature of creation is one.

So when we examine the sayings of many religions, we do so with the premise that they support that, which preceded and succeeded them in the field of rational knowledge and traditions and inherent nature and not with the premise that they are a proof and an original source.[21]

1. The Jewish Religion

Jewish texts affirm the impropriety of bachelorhood considering it a sin and making marriage necessary after the age of twenty. Abortion and infanticide and methods of contraception are also considered a crime and acts of unbelief.

Any woman or wife perpetrating adultery would warrant stoning and the rapist of any married woman would be killed. The rapist of a virgin girl would have to pay a monetary fine and take her as a wife for life for his ill act towards her and those caught in the act of adultery would be killed together.

Anyone slandering a married person without proof would be subject to a fine and punishment.

2. The Christian Religion

In this matter, the Christian religion does not differ from the Jewish religion because Christ came confirming what was in the Torah.[22] Hence Christianity prohibited abortion and placed it on a level with premeditated murder. In the same way, homosexuality was prohibited in the strongest possible terms.

The revolution of morals, which Jesus instigated, was in reality a war against the distortion (of religious texts), dissolution, and degeneracy among the people of Israel.

In the Gospels it says: *'You have heard it said: do not commit adultery. But I say whosoever looks to a woman he desires has committed adultery in his heart, and when your right eye calls you to sin, then pluck it out and throw it from you. For it is better for you to destroy one of your organs than for all of your body to go to Hell*[23]. *'It is said that whosoever divorces a woman; let him give her a document of divorce. But I say that whosoever divorces a woman other than in the case of fornication has exposed her to the possibility of adultery'.*[24]

9

3. In the Religion of Zoroaster

This religion encouraged marriage and building a family and bearing children. In one of its texts it says that 'the married man is greatly preferable to the bachelor and he who supports a family is much more favoured than he who has no family, and he who has children is even more favourable than that.'[25]

Elsewhere it says that 'every time the number of children of a man increases, his closeness to his Lord increases.'[26]

Parents used to organise the marital affairs of those of their children who had reached the age of adolescence, it not being acceptable for a man to remain unmarried. Also any occupation or work which would distance the individual from the family was unacceptable.

Among them, divorce was not approved of except in the case of barrenness, or adultery, or infidelity to the state of married life. Amongst their laws was the prohibition of masturbation, which could be punished by flogging. The consequences for one who committed adultery, or homosexuality, or lesbianism, was death. Likewise, the punishment for abortion among them was execution.

4. Buddhism

In Buddhism, the punishment for an adulteress was to be publicly thrown as prey to the dogs. As for her partner in the crime, he would be roasted alive on a red-hot bed of steel.

Looking at a woman with desire decreased ones vows and the lustful glance stripped one of one's intellect.

5. Confucianism

The ancient Chinese considered the holding back of a man from marriage to be a character deficit and a crime against the ancestors and the state which could not be excused, even for religious men.

They used to delegate a special official whose work was to make sure that every man of age thirty was married and that every woman was married before the age of twenty.

One of the sayings of Confucius says 'if a house stands on a firm foundation then the world is safe and sound'.

Conclusion

After that brief summary of the family system among various civilisations and religions, it is clear that all of humanity agrees upon the call for marriage and procreation as an extension of the human species, and upon the impropriety of the unmarried state and the unlawfulness of fornication and infidelity etc. This concord from the peoples of humanity shows its truthfulness and intrinsic naturalness. Islam, obviously, does not accept a great number of the rules and punishments of these ways of life and civilisations, but our concern is the whole picture and the points of concord only.

Marriage in Materialistic Societies

Despite the obvious harmony of human nature regarding the establishment of the family and married life, and that there is no structure to the human species without this establishment and the fortification of its elements, one can observe certain voices calling for that which goes against the current of intrinsic human nature, and denies this law of the existence, and so just as disrespect towards and neglect of the law of the atom has occurred, so mockery is made of the existence of the family. Whilst the system of the universe has its own direct and natural reaction through radioactivity, the family and society despite its not having a direct and instantaneous natural reaction[27], has a greater and more severe effect after the passage and elapse of time.

Among the most important of the slogans, which have gone outside the law of nature, are those said by Marx, Freud, and Durkheim. Freud made the sexual impulse the basic factor in the development of mankind, while Marx considered it to be Economics, and Durkheim went for the social factor. The proof of the invalidity of these philosophies is first and foremost that they are mutually contradicting in addition to the fact that the pressures which surrounded society helped to create them. The severe pressure which society faced from those who called themselves religion, and the grave contradiction that appeared between the words and deeds of the religious authorities is but one example. Another example is the imposition of legal codes which go against human nature like the church's prohibition of divorce, and the inquisition and extreme quelling of any opposition together with the social gulf between the elite and nobility and the poor and miserable. All these matters have fuelled these philosophies.[28]

Section Two

The Call of Nature[29]

Marriage as a Necessity

Marriage is a vital necessity. The survival of the species depends upon it and the survival of any organism is an intellectual necessity. Hence the world's intelligentsia try to prevent the extinction of a particular organism. So what of humanity? The Qur'an states:

'But when he turns his back, his aim everywhere is to spread mischief in the land and to destroy crops and progeny, but Allah loves not mischief'.[30]

In the matter of destroying progeny there is no difference between active destruction and passive destruction. Qur'anic verses and prophetic traditions stress marriage as being mandatory for the common good and recommended for the individual good.

This is from one angle. From another, were it not for marriage, humanity would suffer from some extremely harmful diseases, as medical science has proven, and the avoidance of any possible harm is mandatory both from a religious and an intellectual point of view. From another angle again, a person to deny himself, in moderation, of the good things in life is also intellectually and religiously wrong as the story of 'Ala shows in '*Nahj al-Balagha*'.[31] In a well-known case, the Prophet himself stopped a man who had vowed to abstain (from all the good things in life including marriage) by the saying '*There is to be no monasticism in Islam*'.[32]

It may be argued that the Qur'anic verse: '*The monasticism which they innovated was not prescribed by Us for them, (We commanded them) only to seek the good pleasure of Allah*'[33], contradicts this. However it should be pointed out that the rule was temporary in the face of an overflow of Jews in the world, and therefore Islam abrogated the rule. As for bringing together '*they innovated it*' and '*we did not make it incumbent upon them*', it is clear that they innovated it firstly, and then Allah ratified it.

13

Early Marriage

The custom of early marriage is upheld by the intellect and the religion. It was the norm amongst Muslims from the dawn of Islam up to and before the cultural, economic, and military assault by the laws of the West and East upon their lands. If this (early marriage) had not been the case, then it would have led either to depravity, the least form of which is masturbation, or to illness as physicians have shown.

It was the custom of Muslims to marry off girls from the age of ten to fifteen or thereabouts, and boys from attaining maturity up to age eighteen. Early marriage was a vital necessity for them because of its simplicity. There was no condition of completing studies or military service. Marriage was like food and drink and clothing to them. A certain man would need a certain woman and vice versa, and nothing would prevent them from coming together in lawful matrimony.

The West, in placing obstacles and hurdles in the way of marriage, has laid itself open to public and private licentiousness as well as various other perversions. Its own figures show that most youngsters are sexually active from age ten for girls and from reaching physical maturity for boys, with all the dangerous consequences of that such as abortion and the profusion of illegitimate children found on the streets and in the slums, as well as various sexually transmitted diseases, and adulterous acts together with marital and family infidelity and incest and suicide, the appearance of homosexuality, and the trade in buying and selling children and so on.

Knowing that Islam is the religion of human nature, it is clear that sexual purity and cleanliness necessitates that we return to the teachings of Islam in this important area of life.

It should not be argued however: Why did the Messenger of God not marry until the age of twenty-five and for that matter 'Ali, because it can be said that one reason may be that the Prophet was poor, his family suffering great hardship as is seen in the story of the dividing up of the sons of Abu Talib. As for 'Ali, he was at the most serious stage in facilitating mankind's transition from darkness to light. It is clear that in this state, a man sacrifices everything for the sake of his goal.

Simplicity of Dowry

The Prophet has said: '*The best of women in my community is she of the most radiant of face and the least of dowry*'.[37]

This is common sense more than tradition, for it is the needs of the young men and women which lead them towards marriage and the dowry is no more than symbolic. There should be nothing to prevent two souls from coming together in a legal way no matter whether their conditions are poor or rich, especially as we see now certain nations making the dowry incumbent upon the man and others making it upon the woman and others still leaving it out altogether.

Islam sanctions the dowry out of honour and respect for the wife but it is not to be over done, rather it stresses the simplicity of the dowry so that it is enough for the husband to teach the wife a chapter from the Qur'an or a simple craft, or even give her a plain iron ring.

Then on, it is clear that after the marriage, the two will be motivated towards working and earning, because the person who knows that he has a responsibility will run towards life as opposed to one who does not feel any responsibility.

Simplicity of dowry made for the best women of the nation according to the Prophet because it makes this vital element of life easier and quicker. '*God wants for you ease and he does not want difficulty*.'[38] It is related that the Prophet said: '*Make things easy upon yourselves and do not make things difficult*.'[39] Ease in anything promotes the absence of stress on the person physically and mentally.

As for the 'most radiant of face', perhaps this stems from good moral behaviour which promotes the radiance of the face and skin.[40]

In this way, it was the custom amongst Muslims, before the age of Western materialism, for the dowry to be small and simple, except in a very few cases, for the 'Umayyad and 'Abbasid caliphs diverged from the traditions of Islam to the traditions of the Persian kings and the Caesars in every domain and especially in the matter of dowries. Because of this, the impeccable Imams used to emphasise and insist upon the dowry of the *sunna* - that practised by the Prophet.

The Parents' House

Muslim society, before the attack of materialism, used to marry off its sons and daughters, and both parties - the parents and the children - were satisfied and content with the parents house as an abode for the newly-weds, without distinguishing between whether the house belonged to the parents of the bride or of the groom. The couple would live in one of the rooms of the house and everyone would contribute to the income, work and affairs of the household.[41] Because of this, marriage was simple and easy regarding housing and furniture and assistance, and the new couple would learn from the older ones various aspects of life.

Others would live in a new house whose land was free according to the law '*the land belongs to Allah and whoever lives upon it*'[42]. The methods of construction were simple and humble, and there were no governmental difficulties such as taxes or planning permission or the like.

I still recall that the people at the Holy city of Karbala were almost one hundred thousand in number and upon analysis; we would not find more than four unmarried men among them. Today however, the situation is quite the opposite. Society has collaborated with the state, which lays down false laws in this respect. But wherever there is no steadfastness and no organisation in exercising sexual capacity, it becomes distorted and perverse.

It is necessary - if we desire happiness - to re-balance society, and to return to the Qur'anic verse: ' *He releases them from their heavy burdens and the yokes that were upon them*'.[43] So that there will no longer exist any social burdens or legal fetters, and therein lies the happiness of Muslims in this world and the next.

16

Simplicity of Requirements

The saying of the Prophet *'the least of them in dowry'*[44] includes all possessions. If the custom present in certain countries now and as was usual among the earlier Muslims, of the couple being satisfied with their belongings before the wedding then this would doubtless be an important factor in decreasing the level of non-marriage and corruption.

My father told me that they used to live in Samarra in a single house, and when his sister got married, the gift was very humble, not exceeding a new dress, which her husband bought for her. On the night of the marriage the bride moved to the room of the groom and the matter was concluded.

I actually saw them myself. Theirs was the happiest of households and they produced fine children and grandchildren.

Contentment is a treasure that never runs out, and contentment with reality, without the vain excesses and exaggerations, which usually surround things, causes mental and physical comfort.

History records the dowry of Fatima al-Zahra[45] and the circumstances of her marriage. The dowry was the sum of thirty dirhams according to various versions. The furnishings of her marriage were basic in the extreme so that even the carpet of the room was of sand, as is reported. Despite this it was the happiest of houses not only in the history of Islam but also in the history of humanity.

The messenger of God made this dowry *sunna* and made it the dowry of all his daughters so it came to be known as the dowry of the *sunna*. However, stealth and bravery are required from educationalists and in Islamic circles, and from parents so that they can do away with these man-made laws and detrimental customs.

17

Section Three

The Married Couple and Conditions, Rights, and Customs

Religion and Morals

The noble Prophet has said: '*If one comes to you whose religion and morals please you then marry them*'[46].

This criterion that the prophet has mentioned is the criterion of common sense also. Naturally the person must be able to provide for his family if the wife so needs, just as he should not be an invalid particularly with a venereal disease or that, which incapacitates him from fulfilling the sexual needs of the wife.

If the behaviour of either of the married couple is not good, the house becomes like a hell, and if one or other of them does not have a code of conduct, which keeps them from wrongdoing then the man, might even be prepared for his wife to become a prostitute. Religion and morals can be judged from previous behaviour, and as to whether he or she is capable of bearing children can be known from the relatives[47] and from certain medical checks.

As for beauty, wealth, position, and social status and so on, they are not in the least bit essential (impossible as not everyone is beautiful and wealthy).

As for age, for if the balance of Islam in marrying every widow and widower is looked at then no fault could be found in either comparing age or neglecting to do so although it is probably better to pay attention to this element also. Hence the Qur'anic reference to the People of Heaven as '*equal in age*'.[48]

Hence we still see, even in this age, that this is the custom of many Muslims although it was more prevalent in the past when it was Islamic.

19

The wearing of the veil for women is also part of the religion as is restraint by men from practising forbidden acts, particularly in this material age with its voracious appetite for lust and seduction.

Means of Subsistence

There is no doubt that being able to expend to run the household is one of the most important matters of married life. Allah states in the Qur'an: *'If they are poor then Allah will enrich them from His bounty'.*[49]

This is correct one hundred percent. This is because the unmarried man does not have the motivation to earn money in the same way that the man who feels a responsibility does. This in addition to the fact that it is a matter from the unseen world as is everything we see in this world; it has its apparent cause and its real cause which is the will of Allah.

However, despite this, a means of subsistence should be acquired including place of abode and other needs. Islam has laid down laws in this respect like *'the land belongs to Allah and whoever develops it'*[50], or *'whoever attains something which no other Muslim has first attained then he has the greater right to it'.*[51]

Therefore it is possible that a charitable organisation could build simple homes on land with wells or the like for general water and rainwater tanks for drinking water, with an orchard for fruits and vegetables and rearing animals. Then they could be leased which would make things very simple for housing and food and also clothing which could be made from the wool of the animals reared in the house. If there were someone in the house who could sew or perform another task for the family then that would be enough to cover half the expenses. The other half could be obtained by work, which also promotes physical and mental health, self-satisfaction and independence from others.

So if God blesses us with manufacture and agriculture and we have water and earth and willing hands, we will have become independent from others. As 'Ali said: *'Become independent from whoever you wish and you will become his equal*.[52]

Equality

Islam has made the Muslim man an equal to the Muslim woman.
This tenet was in effect in Islamic lands until the appearance of
nationalisms and geographical borders which were artificially created
by the West to split up the Muslims and their country. These two
tactics were adopted by various dictatorial rulers to assist them
towards more despotism and more provinces for their sponsors who
put them into power in the country on the condition that they
implement their decisions, as well as the fact that this completes their
deception.

I remember that the people coming to Iraq from India, Pakistan,
Afghanistan, and Iran, from the Gulf, Syria and Lebanon used to
marry amongst each other and with Iraqis and vice versa. The same
was true of any land transactions even after the fall of the
aforementioned rules of land and precedence.

Colonialism and its agents set out to demolish the laws of Islam and
replace them with their own laws.

With the same ease as marriage and selling took place, so did buying
and obtaining free goods such as salt and fish and the like. The same
can be said for freedom of movement without passport, there being
no geographical borders, along with all the other tenets of Islam that
have been gradually eroded. At that time there was no barrier to any
of the Islamic freedoms nor was there any tax on anything.

In any case, it is imperative that Muslims concern themselves, except
in cases where they are compelled by force of arms, with bringing
back the laws of Islam in every aspect of their lives. This includes the
condition of equality between the married couple as stated by Islam
and has been shown by the jurists in their explanatory books and
their practical essays. Then the darkness may be lifted gradually just
as it came to our lands gradually.

Abolition of Conditions

It is imperative that all man-made conditions which have no connection with Islam are abolished from the marital agreement.

Granted, if something is made a condition and it is religiously acceptable then it may be agreed upon by the two parties, but as the saying goes: the more restrictions there are on something the less frequently it occurs.

Every complication lessens the opportunity for marriage whether it be the conditions of the groom or of the bride. It is probable that when a law imposes a condition it seeks to solve a certain problem, but problems are increased from another perspective. For example a law seeking to prevent thieves from stealing by night might impose a curfew.

The basis of marriage in Islam is simplicity and keeping away from complications and un-Islamic traditions and surplus formalities, which are routinely imposed. Among that which simplifies marriage is that no fee is taken for the marriage contract, as was the case in Iraq fifty years ago when the scholars who used to formulate the contracts were prevented from taking payment for discharging their services.[53]

There is no doubt that complexity however small and minor causes delays and in any number add up to a greater delay. Therefore if these matters were abolished along with all the other officialities of which there are an abundance these days, marriage would become easy and would be popular among young men and women as well as divorcees and so on.

The Couple's Happiness

The principle that *'people have dominion over their wealth and their own selves'* is an important one Islamically.[54] The West has progressed and flourished relative to the extent it has practised it. Muslims have regressed whenever they have neglected and ignored it.

This principle must be applied to the married couple. They are, together, free in the choices they make in everything that God has permitted. The only exception which many scholars have noted is in the rights of the virgin girl if her father or paternal grandfather are living, in which case she is subject to their opinion and requires their permission to marry. When the giving of permission is feasible and no other secondary principle applies, then her wishes should be satisfied and permission given.

Similarly, it is not at all conceivable that the young man or woman should be compelled to marry a certain person. Not only is this against the sacred law and common sense, it very often causes problems, the least of which are separation, estrangement and divorce, and in some cases can reach the level of murder and suicide as is common today.

What place is there for compulsion in the relationship of marriage the meaning of which is the intimate companionship of husband and wife by day and by night at home or abroad, and throughout all the circumstances and mental states of each party?

Therefore the marriage of the two must arise out of mutual agreement and no one should have the right to force them to marry.

Idolatry of Traditions

There are certain traditions that have become so widespread as to be now generally accepted as if they were God given laws whereas they do not in reality have any connection with Islam. They are in fact contradictory to the laws of God. The idolatry of customs and the prevalence of deviations is a major problem which faces almost every country. Hence, the necessity arises for visionaries and academics to undertake a courageous stand against this crippling malady and to point out its weaknesses.

These traditions at times assume a holy nature which can make the people all the more ready to believe them and put them into practice. It is not proper either from a religious or intellectual standpoint to pay attention to the compatibility of star signs of the husband or the wife, and although it is correct that a marriage taking place when the moon is in Scorpio will not be joyous, even this may be eliminated through supplication, Qur'anic verses or almsgiving.

There are also certain foreign customs that have reached the Islamic world which observe that the married couple should not be related in any way. This is not correct as can be seen in the marriage of 'Ali and Fatima and certain of the Imams and their sons. It is related that the Emissary of God looked to the children of 'Ali and those of 'Aqueel saying *'Our daughters are for our sons and our sons are for our daughters'.*[55] Indeed, the habit of Muslims from the beginning of Islam was to marry between cousins on the mother's and father's side. (This is based on the fact that Allah Almighty has condoned and encouraged cousin marriage as it is evident from the holy Qur'an,
"O Prophet! Verily We have made lawful for you your wives whom you have given their dowry . . . and the daughters of your paternal uncle, and the daughters of your paternal aunts, and the daughters of your maternal uncle, and the daughters of your maternal aunts . . ."
Chapter 33, verse 50.)

Whatever the case may be, Islamic standards should not be mixed up with Western standards.

The Rights of the Married Couple

The husband has no right over his wife other than the conjugal right, and in the matter of her exit from the house for purposes other than in fulfilling her duties[56] since: *'No creature should be obeyed at the cost of disobedience to the Creator'.*[57]

These rights are brought together in the following Qur'anic verses:

'And women shall have rights similar to the rights against them according to what is equitable'.[58]

'They are your garments and ye are their garments'.[59]

'But men have a degree over them'.[60]

There is absolutely no right for the husband to transgress with regards to his wife, especially as the marriage has taken place with her consent and with her ability to make conditions and that she has certain rights over the wealth of the man if he divorces her as well as other choices which are at her discretion. She also has the right to make the condition that the man does not marry another beside her, and that she can be the agent in divorcing herself, and that he can not divorce her - as many scholars believe - according to the report that Mansour Ibn Younis said: ' *I said to Abu Al-Hasan that one of my colleagues had a wife whom he divorced so she left him. Subsequently he wished her back but the woman said " I will never marry you until you agree not to divorce me and not to marry another besides me". So Abu Al-Hasan asked whether he did so and I said Yes. He said 'He has done ill'. Then he said 'But now, tell him that the condition should stand, for the Emissary of Allah has said, "The Muslims should stand by their personal conditions".*

This was related by Sheikh Murtada in *Al-Makasib*. Further detailed study of the *hadith* and pronouncements of the jurists can be found in the book of Fiqh.[61]

Section Four

Islam's Word on the New Born Child

The Fruit of Marriage

The goal of marriage is the maintenance of human kind so it is important that the two parents pay attention to bringing up the children after marriage or even before it, as in the saying: '*Choose well for your seed, for what is bred in the bone comes out in the flesh*'. Whether it be that the man chooses a fine mother or the woman chooses a good father, the child will take after each of them. Then comes the time for impregnation, the method for which Islam makes plain. Then the period of pregnancy and suckling where it is recommended that it be undertaken by a beautiful woman for 'beauty delights'. After that comes upbringing and education and the age of studying, from kindergarten until university. Similarly, care must be taken in choosing a name for them as in the saying '*nomen est omen*' and as has been proven by psychology. Hence, the Prophet of Islam used to change ugly names to good ones.

The prevalence of children born with deformities, diseases, incapacities and mental deficiencies in the Islamic world in the last half of the twentieth century is one of the unpleasant results of Western lifestyle which has overcome the Muslims with all kinds of poisons and anxieties and corrupt habits from fashions and cosmetics to foodstuffs and certain chemical medicines and so forth.

I myself do not recall, before the second world war, even one instance of any of these terrible occurrences in infants where we used to live in Karbala and Najaf when Iraq was living in a state of Islam. Today however, hardly a day passes without us hearing of a case or cases of abnormalities of this sort.

As for the cure, although it lies in the complete restoration to life of Islam, prevention gives a clear and effective result in reducing these diseases.

The Importance of Health

The married couple must place a great importance on hygiene because of the Qur'anic verse: '*save yourselves and your families from the fire*'[62], and because of the saying of Al-Sajjad: '*Your body holds a right over you*'. The human being has a responsibility for his body before Allah as well as for the deeds he has done and their effect on later generations. Illness is rife, particularly in this age where the rules of hygiene have been destroyed in food, drink, clothing, transport, and housing, together with travel from cold climates to hot climates and vice versa. Modern technology has destroyed a large part of health, while new modes of dealing with life have destroyed another part, and foods and drinks a third part.

Similarly it is imperative that sexual health be maintained where an excess of intercourse and bathing is one of the most detrimental things to the health as Avicenna said: 'Stay continent (of semen) as far as you can for it is the water of life to be poured into the womb'. Likewise, a paucity of sexual intercourse has its own ills proven by medical science, so the best is to opt for moderation and the middle course.

It is also important to observe the times for intercourse[63] as is found in the major works and mentioned by physicians. This particularly during times of pregnancy when many ills can be directed to the foetus which can result in its death, deformity or suffering from chronic disorders.

Hence we see a prevalence of physical and mental disorders in children. This stems from many causes including unhealthy parents and exposure of the child to ills. Children then are now being born at a time when exposure to diseases and problems is increasing, while mankind is responsible before Allah for his children, as is reported reliably.

Suckling

There is no doubt that the best nourishment for the child is the mother's milk as is confirmed by the religion and by medical science[64], except when an infectious disease or the like strikes the mother. One of the reasons for the prevalence of diseases in the child and in the mother is feeding something other than the mother's milk to the child. It harms the new born because his metabolism is not prepared for anything other than his mother's milk and so causes many types of illnesses as is witnessed these days. It also harms the mother because the body after childbirth prepares for breast feeding which, if it does not take place, can cause the milk to become clotted and coagulated in the breast, in addition to the dangers of non-secretion of surpluses in the body which are intended to be discharged through their proper channels. Furthermore, the breast that does not feed tends towards sagging which can lead to a decline of its beauty which is a loss where the woman who has a partner is concerned. Beauty is beloved in religion, common sense and in customs, as in the *hadith*: '*God is beautiful He loves beauty*'[65], and other examples. The intellect weighs up each quality of perfection and beauty is one of the parts of perfection. As for custom, it is too obvious to mention.

It is recommended that the natural mother should feed the child whilst in a state of ritual purity because the milk passes to the soul and to the body as is proven in the religion and in medicine. Hence if the father is forced to feed the child by one other than the child's natural mother, then it is recommended that he choose a woman of good qualities according to the details laid out by scholars.

Upbringing and Protection

It is necessary for the parents to protect the children from deviancy in morals and values. Protecting is incumbent religiously, as in the Qur'an: '*Protect yourselves and your families from the fire*'.[66]

In previous times, before modern methods, and before the colonialist networks had spread through Islamic lands, sons used to follow in the footsteps of their fathers except in a very few cases. In this age however, deviancy is the norm. The majority of youngsters today, despite their young ages and lack of experience, and with their deviant modes of thinking propagated by colonialist factions and organisations, view their parents as reactionary and superstitious, whilst they themselves have been seduced by the propaganda networks and mass media in the country which promote every forbidden thing from alcohol to gambling, licence and perversion. The immature youngster by his nature and inexperience burns with vitality, activity, desire for change, and lust and is thus quickly attracted towards deviancy.

Hence arises the necessity of a thorough concern for the children from parents, relatives, and society as a whole. For without direction, harm and corruption will not only strike the children but will become general amongst their families and entire communities.

The forces of Saddam in Iraq, and the Communist forces in Afghanistan and the like have cost these countries a lot of blood and tears. This is true of many of the other Islamic lands where many lives have been sacrificed at their hands.

When we say 'protection of children', we don't simply mean advice and guidance, but as well as that we mean making them feel part of a healthy environment and preparing for them the means of obtaining work and making a living, and forging links for them with a mosque or a school or a library or a religious community centre, and marrying them when they come of age and seeking gainful employment for them.

The Bond of Kinship

Kinship has a prominent role in safeguarding society from deviance. The married couple may not be related in any way so kinship develops through their children, among themselves and between them and the parents' relatives.

Kinship is a very important means of reaching a common understanding and of strengthening the bonds of friendship and co-operation, of solidarity and mutual regard.

The parents should sow the seeds of this in their children so that they may derive benefit from it and also give benefit. For in kinship there is benefit gained and given, rights and responsibilities, give and take. The rewards in it are unfathomable.

In the Qur'an comes the words: '. . . *and be careful of (your duty to) Allah, by whom you demand one another your rights, and to the bonds of kinship*'[67].

Here the bond of kinship and guarding against breaking it are linked with piety and God-consciousness and guarding against disobeying Him.

There are many reports about this matter. The Prophet has said: ' *The bond of kinship populates the houses and increases life spans even if the inhabitants are not good people*'[68].

Imam Al-Baqir has said: '*The bond of kinship purifies deeds and makes wealth grow. It keeps tribulations at bay and increases longevity*'[69].

Imam Al-Sadiq has said: '*The bond of kinship improves the character, cleanses the hands, perfumes the soul, increases sustenance and adds to longevity*'[70].

In another report from Imam Al-Sadiq comes that a man came to the prophet and said: '*Messenger of God, I have a family and I was their head but now they bring me pain and I wish now to disown them*'. *The Prophet said 'Then God will disown you all'. The man asked 'What shall I do then?' 'The prophet said 'Give to he who denies you, bond with he who cuts off from you and forgive whoever wrongs you. If you do this, God will be your backer*'[71].

A child disobeying and disrespecting his parents, religiously prohibited and intellectually detestable, is a form of breaking the bond of kinship. Similarly a father's disrespect to his children - which is also disrespect and is referred to in traditions - is also a kind of breaking this bond.

When a person is born he is surrounded by a plethora of rules and etiquettes, as well as by universal laws and practices. Therefore a person should prepare himself to adapt in a practical way to these rules and etiquettes and to follow those laws and traditions. Otherwise he will find himself to be the first casualty because of the clash he will experience coming up against them and in many cases he may also cause harm to others besides him.

Virtues and Non-violence

Supposing that a man had a number of wives long term, or if he became a widower or his marriage was annulled or he became divorced, he should not place the status of one wife above the other, nor should he place the children of one wife over those of another. This can cause the break-up and dispersion of the family in many cases, and can sow the seeds of enmity and hatred amongst the children. In extreme cases this can end up in injury, beating, murder and suicide.

The wives must also not be jealous of one another[72] for this also propagates enmity and all its consequences including murder, especially if one wife has children while the other does not.

These kinds of enmities and quarrels as well as being disobedience to God which warrant punishment in the afterlife also disturb the serenity of life without good reason.

Some friends of mine who have visited parts of Asia and Africa and certain Western countries have told me that the concepts held by some Muslims of hatreds and enmities and quarrels and their consequences are generally not present there.

Human nature often calls for these things but the consequences of them is obvious if a person uses his intelligence and strengthens his faith in God and desires His reward and fears His punishment.

A good upbringing and the development of an environment of tolerance and loving and non-violence are the best way in manifold areas of life. Hence the parents should school themselves and their children in noble morals and praiseworthy virtues and non-violence in marital matters so that they may find happiness in this world and the next.

Section Five

Problems and Safeguards towards Maintaining Harmony

The Happy Household

Married life can vary greatly from couple to couple. One couple can make their home heavenly and happy through morals and virtues, good habits and sympathetic behaviour.

Another couple however, can be found to be the opposite of this, one or both of them being uncouth, violent and bad mannered or with bad habits whether it be smoking in the vicinity of the other person which can cause friction, or to be indiscreet and not to say anything, or by eating pungent foods like garlic, onions, and leeks.

It is perhaps a familiar sight to see husbands fleeing from their homes to avoid their ill-mannered wives and vice versa when the wife occupies herself in a certain activity in order to avoid her husband.

The humanistic and Islamic view of society is that each of the married couple should respect and be aware of their partner's needs in their life and realise that they are also a human being with emotions, feelings and sensitivities and that any ill-mannered behaviour can cause pain and in many cases ends up in divorce and separation.

It is important that each partner wherever possible should overlook the slip-ups and mistakes of the other just as the prophet has ordered.

I myself once saw an ill-charactered man drive his wife to death and his second wife followed her.

The person of bad character is generally driven by his behaviour towards bad consequences, while good character and morals usually lead to good consequences. This is the principle involved which the prophet made clear.

There is no doubt that human natures vary in goodness and badness. However, the effect upon the person of education and self-development cannot be denied. A person should educate himself in good personal relationships with others, as is mentioned in the Qur'an in the verse: '. . . *good fellowship*'[73].

Maintaining an atmosphere in the household where no one party forces the other to work in the house or for the house can make the household peaceful and happy. Compulsion though can make the house into a hell on earth which can destroy all the occupants including any children there may be.

No to Extravagance!

The married couple should avoid in particular extravagance and profligacy.

The difference between the two is that the former is to do with excess where the necessity remains in principle, while the latter is expenditure that is not necessary in the least.

In the Qur'an comes an indication that the seriousness of the second type is greater in the words: '*Spendthrifts are akin to devils*'[74], whereas this kind of seriousness has not been said of extravagance.

In a *hadith* it is said '*Pouring out excess water and discarding a date is extravagance*'[75].

Certain laws relating to this subject have been highlighted in 'The Book of Food and Drink' in 'The Encyclopaedia of Fiqh'[76].

In another Hadith is said: 'God is merciful; to he who knows his capacity and does not transgress his limit'[77].

The lively society is one which makes use even of its refuse. Regarding the Qur'anic verse: '*God will revive the dead*'[77], the probable meaning is that they are of no use until God revives them and they become of the living.

At times, there may be a sense of competitiveness between the partners or between two families. This causes many evils, much to the delight of Satan, including extravagance, wastage and ostentation to the level of excess.

Imam 'Ali once gave a ruling that camel meat slaughtered as a form of 'one-upmanship' between two tribal leaders was forbidden and it was left to the scavengers. Perhaps the point is that getting the message across is more important than leaving the meat for the scavengers, even though the meat was slaughtered in a lawful manner.

In any case it is important that the married couple co-operate together from the outset with a view to creating a family whose basis is love and affection and whose driving force is purposefulness and reality, not squandering and extravagance, false facade and idle boasting.

Work Within the Household

Manual work within the household is a blessing which is necessary for psychological well being and beneficial for the body because it leads to health and well being.

It is then important that the married couple should concern themselves with handiwork, and that each one choose for themselves some task or they both undertake it together.

We can still remember the days when families use to work in their houses or outside in the garden or in the fields or the farmyards when people used to live a life of self-sufficiency not being in need of outsiders.

I myself remember the problems that the world experienced after World War II and the famine that struck humanity as a result of those wars. However, Iraq and certain other Islamic countries were not as affected by the famine due to their reliance upon their own produce. At that time, all needs were satisfied internally, and we did not need to import more than white sugar and some cloth. People used to make their own clothes on simple looms and didn't need imported cloth in any great measure. Our father[78] (May the mercy of God be upon him) used to tell us to take our tea with dates or molasses whenever we needed sugar. Then, the entire imports of Iraq did not exceed 30 million Dinars, as all our needs were met from within the country.

These days however, after the flood of oil wells, these imports have reached tens of billions of Dinars but look at the state of Iraq, and the state of the people. One glance at the problems, poverty and hunger which is sweeping the country is enough to confirm the reality.[79]

Therefore a gradual independence from outsiders must be worked towards, through for example making the house into a workstation for the married couple.

It is also important that charitable organisations help provide opportunities for married couples and facilitate and stimulate work for them.

Section Six

Challenges Facing the Family and Society

Divorce Yesterday and Today

It was usual in Islamic countries for marriages to take place in a context of common sense and compatibility. It was the family who would find the appropriate partner with regard to religion, moral behaviour, financial status and physical character. For this reason, marriages on the whole were successful.

The family's choosing for their offspring did not negate the choice and contentment of the prospective couple but rather confirmed it and steered it in the required direction, because of the families knowledge and links to other family circles was more than that of the young man or woman. Further more, the family by possessing a means of exerting pressure on those who wished to divorce could act to prevent splits taking place. Hence the families acted in truth as a kind of safety valve against the recklessness and haste of youth as in the Qur'anic verse:

'Then appoint two arbiters, one from his family, one from hers; if they seek to set things to rights then Allah will cause their reconciliation[80].

This God granted success as with everything else that He causes in this world must be preceded by human action, for God has disdained to run affairs other than through their causes.

I have been told by one of the persons responsible for marriage and divorce in the city of Karbala forty years ago that he only presided over the divorce of one person a year. Today however, now that society has taken up with Western values or has plunged into Westernisation and the misplaced imitation of its laws and customs, it is the youngsters who choose their partners in isolation and without consulting their parents. It is evident now that the criteria for

39

marriage is a mixture of emotion, sexual fervour, inexperience, and immaturity. This is fuelled by the pressure of such values and their false notions of freedom and its attack on authentic customs which it describes as being reactionary or backward and senile. Hence a large proportion of marriages now end in separation and divorce.

For those that fall into these traps the calamities are great.

For these reasons it is imperative that we return to the Islamic lifestyle of happiness which our forefathers lived in the lands of Islam until half a century ago.

Conciliation is Best

The prevalence of divorce in the latter half of this century[81] is attributable to a number of reasons including:

1. A short sighted and arbitrary way of choosing a partner for life because of emotions and the like.

2. A tendency towards over expectation by one partner of the other and an excess of idealising.

3. The pressure of man made laws limiting real freedoms, opportunities for work, travel and obtaining free goods and so on.

4. The spread of exhibitionism, social mingling, licence and dissipation, whereby a man can find someone apparently more beautiful than his wife and a woman can find a man more preferable than her husband.

5. The decline of the restraint promoted by religion and morals and a moving away from the Islamic way.

However, this notwithstanding, it is imperative that marital problems be solved without resort to divorce, for divorce is described as being the most detestable of all that God has made lawful.

The emissary of God has said: *'There is no permissible thing more beloved in the sight of God than marriage, nor is there any permissible thing more detestable in the sight of God than divorce'*[82].

Imam Al-Sadiq has said: *'God loves the house in which there is matrimony and hates the house in which there is divorce for there is nothing more detestable in the sight of God than divorce'*[83].

In another tradition from Imam Al-Sadiq he commands: *'Marry and do not divorce for the heavenly throne verily shakes as a consequence of divorce'*[84].

Why then has God not outlawed divorce altogether?

The answer is that the home may have become an unbearable hell on earth. Alternatively, many things may add up to make reconciliation impossible.

In the case of the Christian church when it forbade divorce, millions of men and women remained partner less, after finding their natures incompatible. Hence corruption and licence and perversity flourished as each partner found, in the air of poisonous freedoms promulgated by the West, all manner of means to prostitution and adultery put in front of them while the media and advertising egg them on.

There is no doubt that if there were present in society institutions dedicated to conciliation and trained conciliators together with charitable bodies, these problems which cause damage to the family, harm the children and come between relatives and at times end up in murder and suicide would certainly reduce.

Certain divorce lawyers who do not heed God and do not experience any barrier from government or society can exploit the will of one of the partners to separate. He then fills his coffers at the expense of religion, conscience and morals. If he were to heed God however he would make haste to resolve matters between them, as in the Qur'anic verse: *'Conciliation is best'*[86].

Polygamy - A Spurious Crisis

The law of the universe runs according to the perfect balance of pairs, as in the Qur'anic verse: *'We have created of everything in pairs so that perhaps you may take heed'*.[87]

However, this does not necessarily mean equality in terms of numbers but rather compatibility in terms of type, whereby each pair is ensured of fulfilling its natural role in life. For example in the world of ants and bees, the queen capable of procreation is one only, whereas the males which compete with each other for the prize of fertilising her are many. This is true of most of the animal kingdom.

Human beings by virtue of being alive like the remainder of living things in this existence are no exception to this rule. Granted, they have their own particularities but so does every other living thing, and just as the divine will has ensured for human beings perfect compatibility in terms of type, as with the rest of existents, it has also defined and shaped humanity in a way particular to itself whereby fulfilment, concord and continuance are ensured, each having its own proof and wisdom.

Among the teachings of Imam Sadiq to Al-Mafdal Ibn 'Amr are his words: 'Humanity was *not created masculine and feminine except in order to be able to reproduce . . .Had an organism given birth to males only or females only then reproduction would cease and the species would become extinct. Therefore some of the offspring came as males and others as females so that reproduction would continue and not be cut off*'.[88]

Imam Al-Rida, speaking about the prohibition of adultery and of violating the law of nature which was created by God to harmonise with the human species and his needs, said: *'God has prohibited adultery because of the corruption it can cause, from murder to loss of lineage and neglect to the children's upbringing and corruption of inheritances and other forms of corruption'*.[89]

It is possible to posit no more than the following four different marital systems between the two sexes:

1. Complete sexual freedom.
2. Polyandry.
3. Monogamy.
4. Polygamy.

There is no doubt that the first two are both invalid from an intellectual and religious point of view as the preceding report from Imam Rida points out. There only remains the latter two.

Statistics and surveys show that women outnumber men, particularly around the ages of puberty and sexual maturity despite the fact that some statistics in some countries show a relative parity between the sexes.

As to why women should outnumber men, that is one of the secrets of nature. However, its wisdom should not be lost on anyone who reflects upon it.

This phenomenon also gives rise to the fact that women are more long lived in comparison to men, perhaps as men are generally occupied with heavy work which can shorten their lives. Men are more often affected by wars and imprisonment or long absences; which necessitates the right of divorce by their wives in religious law, or by the men if they know that they will not be able to maintain the relationship because of imprisonment or the like.

Furthermore, those who are marrying a second, third or fourth wife are obviously not marrying a woman who is already married but one who is free of a husband.

What then is the intellectual problem with polygamy?

If we do not solve this problem through polygamy, then we will either see women without husbands or we will see them taking lovers both of which are in opposition to the balances of rationale and of nature.

Since the beginning of Islam, and for a long time there was no barrier to polygamy. It was in fact totally normal. Disputes amongst wives were as seldom as disputes amongst sisters or between mother and daughter. Then however, the matter became corrupted; by men through their oppression towards women in the context of polygamy, and by women because of their desire for favouritism and being singled out for benefits. Then the majority of women began to detest the concept of polygamy in many Islamic countries, even though polygamy was practised without mishap in countries like Chad and other African countries.

It is then necessary to adjust this situation so that so many women are no longer condemned to spinster hood which is one of the greatest forms of oppression against women.

If the man were to die, then society should take care to facilitate her marriage to someone else or, in the case of divorce, to try to bring about her return to her former husband where possible as is prevalent in countries practising polygamy.

The Prophet married the greater number of his wives after their divorces from former husbands or after the death of their first husbands as was practised from the beginning of Islam and for centuries onward and is still practised now in certain countries.

Is it not a kind of injustice that a young woman, or one who has lost her husband through divorce or by some accident, should remain single when she is a human being with emotions relating to sex, abode, children and so on. In the main though, the corrupted customs of some people deny her all of this. Customs though if transcended will fall. All that is needed is an agent - a powerful current in society, and an authentic culture - to transcend this situation.

The Crisis of Celibacy

Today in Islamic countries, women are suffering from social oppression since these countries have adopted corrupt foreign traditions in this vital area of life. Society oppresses them by delaying their marriage[90], by preventing their re-marriage after the death of their husbands, or when the numbers of unmarried women are great, or for many other reasons. All of this needs to be transcended and overcome with the return to the land of Islamic tradition which conforms to nature and the intellect. It is also imperative that society be educated in harmonising the characters of the married couple as a precaution against marital breakdown, separation and divorce.

This problem of the abundance of celibates or single women may be solved by charitable organisations and social institutions which specialise in the demands of this crisis and the numerous financial, medical and psychological problems associated with it. A woman who is celibate or unmarried is subject to being exposed to physical and mental illness as medical science has shown. In many cases she may not have any means of subsistence[91] and turns to prostitution or other activities like thieving.

Is it right that a large section of the community remain in this state?

Simplifying marriage together with the practise of polygamy and the application of public funds in solving financial problems and the aforementioned laws of precedence[92] and land[93] adds up to an Islamic solution to this problem. However because of the absence of vital Islamic law there is no alternative to charitable organisations and communal weddings as a way towards solving these problems as much as possible. From drops of water and grains of sand oceans and deserts are formed.

A group of friends of mine in Teheran saw to the marriage of 1000 young couples at the one time. The same thing happened with another group in the Eastern province of the Hijaz when they organised the marriage of 300 people.

It is clear that: 'The complexity of a task should not prevent the attempt of achievable tasks'[94] and 'What is not totally realisable as a whole should not be discarded as a whole.'[95] , these being among the best principles with regard to these matters.

Birth Control; Who is behind it?

The emissary of Allah has said: *'Marry, procreate and proliferate!'*[96]
He also said: *'Marry, procreate and proliferate so that I may be*

proud of you as a nation on the day of judgement even if the child is stillborn'. [97]

These two traditions contain laws albeit in the form of recommendations which like all recommendations should only be neglected in the case of strict necessity. The night prayer for example is a recommended act which does not lose its status as such except through necessity. The same goes for proliferation of offspring.

What is taking place today however, goes against this completely. The idea of proliferation has become foreign amongst Muslims whilst the notion of birth control, previously abominable to Muslims, has taken its place. Even in the most desperate periods of Islamic history [98], no promoter of these ideas which go against the intellect and nature was ever witnessed. It is true that certain rulers used to perpetrate gross acts but the law of Islam was in force - generally - throughout society where the economy was Islamic as was the rest of society. Today however, after the appearance of Western colonialism in our lands everything has been overturned. Forbidden things have become permissible. Gambling is commonplace. Taxes and duties, geographical borders, confiscation of freedoms, oppression and terrorism and prevention from fulfilling the Hajj pilgrimage have become permissible. In this atmosphere of opposition to Islam comes a call from the West for Muslims to practice birth control [99] using the argument of the dwindling economic level of the family and the fall in GNP of the countries concerned which are unable to fulfil their commitments to provide enough schools and hospitals and other social services. At the same time they themselves in the West are encouraging their children to marry early and propagate. [100] This call for marriage and childbearing begins with the instruction of children at primary level upwards. There exists amongst Western leaders a great fear that the European nations are on their way to extinction if the negative trend in population growth continues. They also know that the most important cause of this trend lies in the promotion of birth control which swept through Europe during the 1960's and sowed in the European mindset the notion that having children is an erroneous act. Europeans have continued to carry this notion with them until their birth rate has dwindled.

Today they have rediscovered that the error does not lie in the act of bearing children but in the promotion of birth control.[101] Unfortunately they have exported this call to us after having experienced the tragedy of it themselves. They have come to the Islamic world to call Muslims to birth control.

Let us examine the goals of the West in their call for birth control. The goal is to drive Muslims to decline. In this they have found a most effective and devastating weapon capable of weakening Muslims after the failure of all their other weapons. We wonder why the West does not demand the Jews in Palestine to practise birth control. Why do we not see the Jews paying the slightest heed to this call? Why is the state of Israel strongly encouraging childbirth so that it has become commonplace according to visiting journalists to see pregnant women walking the streets or working in shops or teaching or working as policewomen? Why does the state of Israel prohibit birth control while we Muslims allow it and some of us think that it is compulsory like fasting and prayer. The case of birth control is political propaganda aimed at weakening Muslims. It has no connection whatsoever with economics despite what is said.

We wonder: why birth control? Is it that the laws of Allah have changed in the universe? Have nature and Allah's creation been replaced? Or is it that the laws of Allah apply only to one particular epoch rather than another? Is it because we lack lands or water or resources or opportunities?

The Islamic world comprises vast lands suitable for farming and developing.[102] It also has a great store of water and is furnished with unquantifiable resources and potentials.

It is therefore wrong to bang the drums of birth control when there is no need for it.[103]

Iraq for example, which used to be called 'The Fertile Land' supported 40 million people during the 'Abbasid period according to some historians. Nowadays, Iraq's population is no more than half that figure. A country like Sudan would probably be able to feed the entire African continent from the arable land and water resources it has[104]. The same could be said of the rest of the Islamic lands which own a tremendous amount of agricultural, mineral and oil wealth.

47

Where are these resources going to? Why are these riches stagnating? These are the questions which require answers. This is the problem which needs to be solved. All other problems arise from this problem. The population explosion, the economic crisis, underdevelopment, and the lack of political vision all stem from the tyranny, oppression, dictatorship, and despotism of the rulers, their control over Muslims, and their running of the affairs of the land according to their vain desires and not according to sound planning and the interests of the people.

One such ruler in an Islamic land - Saddam - has, according to some statistics, stolen 300 billion dollars from the people, not to mention the wealth he has destroyed in internecine wars. If we add to that the embezzlements of other rulers across history in Islamic lands then how much of the wealth of Muslims has been squandered on the desires and whims of these rulers?

Where there is someone stealing the people's sustenance he must be called to account and confronted with the problem and told he is a thief and demands made for the return of the peoples wealth to them. We should not demand that the people suffer hunger to tell them to restrain from marriage and having children because there is not enough food to go round.

A large portion of the wealth of Islamic lands has gone to the countries of the West. Statistics show that one-fifth of humanity (those living in the industrialised nations) consume four-fifths of the world's wealth. The remaining four-fifths of humanity - the poor living in what is known as the third world - only consume a mere one-fifth of the world's resources.

Herein lies the catastrophe.

The lack of justice in the world and the neglect of Islamic laws of development like the aforementioned two laws of precedence[105] and ownership of land.[106] The stranglehold of governments and their control over affairs. The excess of bureaucrats who deny people's freedoms. Poor distribution of wealth. The lack of a vociferous opposition. The poor peoples are battered and their nobility destroyed. We are denied a voice, then we are denied food and now today we are told to stop having children. The problem of progeny can be solved within the context of an Islamic system based on justice and pluralism. Through justice, Islam ends poverty and closes the gap between rich and poor, ruler and ruled. Through pluralism, the people are given a strong voice with which to speak freely.

The Islamic view of mankind differs to that of other systems. Some systems see man as a heavy burden and views every newborn child as an unwelcome guest and yet another mouth to feed. Islam however, views man as a vital and active force. The Qur'an sees man as the most powerful creation upon the face of the earth and sees within him the secret of advancement in the world: '...*Man can have nothing but what he strives for; and that his striving will be in sight; then he will be rewarded with a reward complete*'.[108]

Islam sees in each new child as a form of progress and advancement. In the words attributed to Imam 'Ali:

'*Do you think that you are a mere germ? While within you is concealed the greater realm.*'[109]

The prophet sees in every birth a new reason to be proud before the other nations of the world. Even if this child was stillborn and had no life. Was it not he who said: '*Marry, procreate and proliferate so that I may be proud of you as a nation on the day of judgement even if the child is stillborn*'.[110]

The newborn may become a scholar or an inventor or an engineer or anything else. He will add to life his potential for work and add a new value and genius to history. Life is not built by tools and machines but by the efforts of men. Life is not run by computers and satellites but by the intelligence of mankind and every new infant is a new intellect, a new arm and a new step forward. Why then all this fear? Has not Allah promised us and His promise is good and true: '*We shall provide sustenance for them and for you*'.[111]

He has also said: '*Marry those among you who are single, and the virtuous ones among your slaves, male or female: If they are in poverty, Allah will give them means out of his grace*'.[112]

Marriage then eradicates poverty and children are a cause of increased wealth. This is the logic of the Qur'an and the Sacred Law. As for those who believe the opposite of this, believing that marriage and children diminish wealth, then they are far from Allah and the Qur'an and from the logic of the intellect and wisdom.

Section Seven

The Role of Institutions

Who is Responsible?

In the logic of Islam: ' *Each of you is a guardian and each of you are responsible for his guardianship*'.[113]

Each person has a role and responsibility without which society has no basis. Since the family is the nucleus of society and the criterion for its advancement or decline rests with it, then it must have a great role in this guardianship.

Girls of marriageable age, divorcees, widows, marital disputes, and for that matter orphans are all subjects which require careful consideration so that wherever possible their problems may be solved. This may be achieved through facilitating the marriage of single persons or through reconciling those parties who have separated. By taking care of orphans and meeting their material and spiritual needs and giving them a good practical and intellectual education.

In materialistic societies, which includes, in this age, Islamic societies, these problems are widespread[114] and individuals do not receive the attention they deserve.

Hence all those who have faith and hope in Allah and the day of resurrection, and who contemplate the reform of society should concern themselves with assisting women and orphans. The emissary of Allah has said: ' Have mercy on the weak, on women and on orphans'.

Is it not the case that any one of us could be susceptible to these problems? So if we do not have mercy on those less fortunate than ourselves we may not be shown mercy when we or our children are in a similar position and in need. In the Qur'anic verse: ' *Let those (disposing of an estate) have the same fear in their minds as they*

51

would have for their own if they had left a helpless family behind. Let them fear Allah and speak appropriately.[115]

In the prophetic tradition: ' *Have mercy upon those who are on the Earth and He who is in the heavens will have mercy upon you* '[116]

The parents are responsible for themselves and the welfare of their family. Society, including intellectuals and capitalists, is also responsible for supporting its elements and families. The greater responsibility falls on the government and the state.

Marriage Agency

Given that the lives of Muslims are beset by difficulties from every quarter, the foremost of which are related to the family and marriage, and since returning to the equilibrium of nature and Islam takes time before the *status quo* is changed and matters return to their rightful place, then it is imperative, as has been previously mentioned, that marital foundations be set up to facilitate the marriages of single men and women. The sexual impulse and the impulse to start a family are present in both men and women and what stands in the way of this are the artificial problems like housing requirements, furniture, earning a living, mediation between the two parties, and expenses for medicaments and educating the children etc. Primary institutions are needed for the root and basis of marriage and secondary ones for its branches and requirements. It is possible that committees for communal weddings be formed which could assist in the marriages of large numbers of youngsters and could provide a great deal of effort and financial support. *'The hand of Allah is with the group'*[117] as is in the prophetic tradition. There is also a great deal of reward due to whoever works towards the marriage of single Muslims.

The prophetic traditions are full of special mentions of motherhood, childhood and the ill, as well as the fact that it is a requirement of Allah's words to 'help one another in righteousness and piety'[118], as well as that of nature and intellect.

Charitable organisations are among the best solutions to numerous problems relating to the family and society and indeed in any area of life in that they:

a). Stimulate the activities of individuals or similar organisations because they tend to be pluralistic and encourage the activities of others.

b). Can be a source of support for people as the reliance upon a group is greater than that of an individual.

c). The obstinate individual will find no room therein for megalomania.

d). Each individual will be heading in the right direction where there is consultation and a meeting of minds as the most intelligent person is he who combines his mind with those of others.

e). Wherever there is competition between a single group of individuals, each one strives to be 'bigger and better' so that things improve in quality and quantity in a way impossible for a single person working alone to achieve however perfect and sincere he was. The exception to this is only in the case of those 'restrained from error' by Allah. Hence we find that the prophet, himself impeccable, saying: ' Oh people consult me in matters'[119]. and before that in the Qur'anic verses: ' Consult them in affairs'[120], and '. . . those who conduct their affairs by mutual consultation'[121], and '. . . by mutual consent and consultation '[122], and so on. Therefore there is a need for charitable organisations in all areas of life.

In Democratic States

It is true that in Democratic countries, charitable organisations are able to work to their full potential while this is not the case in dictatorships or one-party states where they might be banned or expelled or otherwise limited as was experienced in Iraq under the Republicans from the late 1950's at the time of the coup of 'Abd-al-Karim Qasim until the present day. Similarly in Iran under the Pahlevis.

Communal weddings in Democratic states are a simple matter. There, the government is an institution like other institutions but monitors other institutions in order to stop wrongdoing and to promote the advancement of the country and guard the public interest. The public interest is public in the full meaning of the word, where there are free political parties and proper elections, and not as dictators wish to interpret the public interest. They only see their own interests and hide behind dazzling rhetoric.

The organisation which works towards setting up projects for communal weddings should take advantage of the possibilities open to it in a democratic country where such organisations are able to operate in relative freedom, in the light of multi-party politics, ease of law and media and simplicity of obtaining donations etc.

In dictatorships such as Iraq, such matters are not at all simple and extreme caution must be exercised. Probably it should not be communal as the regime bans or expels these kinds of groups. In fact the regime would probably exploit the reputation of these groups for propaganda purposes. This would be more detrimental to society than the benefit hoped for in marrying people. (*There is no obedience to Allah through disobedience*). In the case of dictatorial governments, people must cut them off and not co-operate with them even in the building of mosques. As Imam Al-Sadiq said: ' *Do not build them even a single mosque*'[123].

Facilitation and Substitution

In the words of the poet: 'Oh my soul fulfil your grief for that which you feared is now a reality.'

The laws of Islam became hidden under the Ottoman and Qajarite rulers and before that under the rulers of Andalucia, the Moghuls and Russia. Today Muslims live in an abyss of poverty, disease, ignorance, backwardness and chaos. How then in the context of the family do we raise the economic level to eradicate poverty? How do we raise health standards to combat illness? How do we free ourselves from ignorance? How can we raise the family's status in society so that it can leave chaos behind?

Individual action is not enough, just as the family is not able to solve its problems alone. There is then a need in the Islamic community for organisations to provide facilities and organisations to institute change.

The first will provide facilities for families by opening schools and hospitals and creating opportunities for employment. Otherwise the children of poor or low-income families will not be able to pay the high fees to enter the universities. Nor will they be able to pay the medical bills of those with chronic diseases. Many is the time that a person has sadly had to sell his house in order to pay to treat his heart disease, or those who do not have a house to sell have died of that or some other disease. At the same time, the rulers are embezzling billions in broad daylight, and anyone who speaks out faces prison, torture, accusations and execution. The poor can barely find a morsel to eat and some families live out their years on nothing more than bread and tea, some of them not tasting meat or fruit for years on end. The instances of this are beyond number and cover all aspects of life. I have seen a scholar sell his personal library to cover the wedding expenses of his son. Facilitative committees are then to some degree useful according to the principle: *'The complexity of a task should not prevent attempting the achievable tasks.'*[124]

The root of the problem lies in the substitution by the West and its agent rulers of the laws of Islam which used to guarantee our vitality and progress in life. *'He calls you to what will let you live'*.[125]

Therefore committees to institute change should be set up to bring back the vital laws of Islam. Otherwise our life will be nothing but strife and oppression, as in the Qur'anic verse: *'But whosoever turns away from the remembrance of me shall find a straitened existence'*.[126]

It is true that the man who says he does not believe in the law of gravity and throws himself from a high place will still find his bones broken. Or the man who says he does not believe in Archimedes principle and throws himself in the sea without knowing how to swim, will still drink water until he dies. The same goes for the laws of society, economics, politics, education and the family as Islam confirms.

In so far as salvation lies in the return of these vital laws, then the remit of the committees for change should be to substitute, law by law, each of the false laws with the correct laws. In this way, Allah may look upon Muslims with compassion and rescue them from the backwardness and confusion they now experience.

Another way of supporting the policies of substitution and facilitation is to form groups to make use of free media and equal rights to implement the aforementioned two groups. Similarly help must be sought from philanthropists and charitable bodies to collect funds to meet people's needs as far as possible.

All of this is possible if the concern and efforts of reformists and committed individuals is combined after which Allah may cause something to happen.

It is clearly possible to benefit from good Muslim businessmen in the facilitation and substitution operation. Traders were previously the jewel in the crown in the change that took place in favour of Islam and Muslims. It is capital, power, and knowledge that direct society towards the better or God forbid the worse.

It appears in the traditions that: ' *Islam was built on three things; the wealth of Khadijah, the protection of Abu Talib, and the morals of the Prophet*'. It is these three that helped to foment the rise of Islam.

In another tradition from the Prophet: ' *There are two groups in my nation which if righteous so will my nation be righteous and if corrupt so will my nation be corrupt. They are the scholars and the leaders.*'
If money is not mentioned in this then it is probably due to the fact that money is secondary to the two other things. As in when Imam Hussein was killed through the power of Zayad, the edict of Shureih, and the wealth of the public treasury which had been directed by the powers that were and the edict towards evil and tyranny.

Muslim traders have the ability to raise the status of Islam and deepen it and maintain it as a barrier against the vast currents over the ages. Islamic charitable institutions be they schools, mosques, shrines, or libraries mostly come from Muslim businessmen. So if they enter the picture, God willing, the change and substitution will become easier.

The aforementioned committees should also take part in planning the development operation. Businesses like agriculture, industry, commerce and heritage may also be able to create those committees in this way. Naturally all arms, drugs, and trade in other forbidden articles should be at all costs avoided for Allah is not obeyed through disobedience.

The Public Treasury

One of the benefits of Islam is the provision of a place for gathering moneys and then spending them on necessary matters. This place is known as the public treasury. The policy of the public treasury is to gather money from the rich and to spend it on the poor. This is alluded to in the tradition of the prophet: ' *I have been ordered to take from the rich among you and give to the poor among you*'.[127]

There are four sources of funds for the public treasury: The Khums, The Zakat, The Jizya, The Kharraj each of which are discussed in detail in the books of jurisprudence. These sources can fulfil the needs of the people and the state making the need for raising public taxes obsolete except in very rare occasions like earthquakes, flooding, famine or drought and this under the supervision of the council of jurists and scholars. The secret to the sufficiency of these four taxes is that Islam places matters in the hands of the people while the responsibility of the state is the supervision and direction of the finances through a small number of specialised officials. This is dealt with in greater detail in other books on the subject. Use must be made of the great potential energies which should be rallied to productive work instead of wasting them in needless bureaucracy where they may be dispensed with. The treasury undertakes to fulfil the public's needs including the needs of those who wish to marry but are poor.

In the event of there being no public treasury as is the situation now in Islamic lands, then the principle of 'that which cannot be fully realised should not be completely neglected' must be put into effect through charitable bodies setting up funds to collect donations and distribute them according to the needs of the public including youngsters who wish to marry.

Conclusion

It is truly sad that ignorance, despotism, and selfishness motivate many Muslims both rulers and ruled to such an extent that some Muslims cannot find even a morsel of food or an abode or a wife and other basic needs. Meanwhile, they are surrounded by the bounties of Allah - earth, sky, light, the riches of nature, and the finest principles known to humanity. But they have neglected the laws of Allah and have been rewarded with these problems and crises which have destroyed their religion and way of life.

What has become of Allah Almighty's words: *'are those who know equal to those who do not know'*[128] ,or His words'. . . *do not take those outside your ranks into your intimacy: they will not fail to corrupt you. They only desire for you to suffer'.*[129] or His words: ' . . .and consult them in the affairs of moment . . .'[130] , or His words: ' . . .so that (wealth) does not merely circulate amongst a rich few . . .'[131]

and so many other verses and traditions? So that now the Muslim stands between two points; *'bemoaning the state of his religion and his way of life'*[132] . Whereas Imam Kashif Al-Ghata when he visited Iran said in the prologue to his book *'I did not see one man or woman either weeping or complaining' (meaning here unnatural weeping or complaining)'.* Similarly I do not recall any of that either in Iraq before the second world war where Muslims were not yet subject to Eastern and Western laws.

Today though after having chosen for themselves to be led by the Western agenda and have become a confirmation of Allah's words: *'But whosoever turns away from the remembrance of me shall find a straitened existence'*[133]

Calamity has struck even the righteous among them according to Allah Almighty's words: ' . . .and fear a trial which may not only affect the wrongdoers amongst you '. . .[134]

I now offer some examples of the oppression and distress which have surrounded Afghanistan, Iraq and the Gulf. These are by way of example only for every Islamic land has been struck by this plague.

A certain party in Afghanistan plants opium for export to neighbouring countries and with the proceeds buys weapons with which to kill the people of the country. In this there are at least five criminal acts:

1) Misuse of the blessings of Allah; good land that should be used for good things is used for evil things.

2) The exploitation of workers and means of production for bad ends instead of for righteous ends.

3) Wastage of wealth on tools of destruction, bloodletting and impoverishment instead of being used for building and construction and the needs of the people.

4) Causing pain to the people and the neighbouring countries that should be safe from the calamities of a neighbour falling into the trap of addiction and corruption.

5) Destruction of the country: the natural result of the aforementioned is the destruction of the country and the humiliation and impoverishment of the people. This though is only the natural result of the type of ignorance that we have mentioned and the abandonment of the laws of God. In the Qur'anic verse: '. . . *and be not like those who have forgotten God and He made them forget their own souls . . .*'[135]

Then the West puts Saddam in place so he can embezzle more than 800 billion dollars worth of Muslim wealth and do with Iraq and its neighbours such murder, terrorising, imprisonment, torture, war, famine, torment, and economic destruction as has not been witnessed in the whole of history.[136] The crimes of the Mongols, the Tartars and the Hajaj pale into insignificance compared to the crimes of Saddam and his party. The West then makes the Iraqi regime into a tool for terrorising and corrupting the Gulf states and their other neighbours so that they ask for military bases on their soil and buy from the West billions of dollars of arms[137] rather than serving the needs of the people and improving the lifestyle of the country. In this way the Islamic community is in the worst possible state of oppression and distress.[138]

There is as we previously said no cure to this other than through a general awareness which is the prelude towards a return to the laws of Islam. For Islam is what will rescue humanity as that Muslim who went to conquer Persia said when Rustum asked him 'What do you want' He said ' We have come to bring the people from obeying other people to obeying Allah and to rescue humanity from the narrowness of the earth to its wideness.

Notes

[1] Mentioned on BBC Television's *Heart of the Matter*, Sunday 28/11/1999, 11.25 p.m. and on *Night Waves*, BBC Radio 3, 26/11/1999, 9.30 p.m.

[2] See *Europe in Figures*, Chapter 18 Fertility.

[3] See *United Nations Demographic Yearbook 1999*, Chapter 9.

[4] The Holy Qur'an: The Tribe of Israel (17): 31.

[5] The Holy Qur'an: The Forgiver (40): 21.

[6] The Holy Qur'an: The Heifer (2): 5.

[1] The Holy Qur'an: The Hajj Pilgrimage (22): 11.

[2] The son's of Marwan refers to the Umayyad Caliphate in the early days of Islam. (Translator's note)

[3] A reference to the 'Abbasid Caliphate. (Translator's note)

[4] The Holy Qur'an: Public Estates (8): 24.

[5] A major book on Qur'anic commentary mentions three possibilities for the identity of 'Dhul-Qarnain' : Alexander of Macedonia, One of the Yemenite Kings, Koroush one of the kings of Iran. The author of the book favours the third possibility because the description fits best Koroush. However the main thing is that he was a 'righteous servant of Allah.' (Tafsiri-Nimoune, vol 12, page 542, Nasir Makarim). (Translator's)

[6] The Holy Qur'an: The Cave (18): 89.

[7] The Holy Qur'an: Public Estates (8): 41 (*'Know that whatever you acquire, a fifth of it is for Allah'*).

[8] The word God is used here for translation purposes more or less interchangeably with the Arabic word Allah (The God, The Deity, The Unseen). However the Islamic conception of God as elucidated in the Qur'an differs from other conceptions in its strict adherence to the belief in monotheism - the oneness of God who has no partner in creation and no sire. He is The One, The Eternal, He does not beget, nor was He begotten and there is nothing like unto Him. (Translator's note)

[9] The Holy Qur'an: The Winnowing Winds (51): 49.

[10] The Holy Qur'an: The Coalitions (33): 72.

[11] The Holy Qur'an: The Romans (30): 30.

[12] The Holy Qur'an: (the letters) Y.S. (36): 36.

[13] The Holy Qur'an: Consultation (42): 11.

[14] See Laws of Hammurabi, Articles 130 - 158.

[15] This was after the age of 25 for men and 20 for women during the reign of Augustus.

[16] They were forfeit certain types of inheritance.

[17] This was during the age of Augustus 30-14 BC.

[18] Al-Hurani has collected lineages and organised them into levels according to the size of each level and he gives them thirteen classifications.

[19] Like monetary fine or banishment or death by stoning, and this appears in the writings of certain of their historians like Akthum bin Saifi.

[20] The Holy Qur'an: Women (4): 22.

[21] This is because those who fabricate lies against God do not bring forward any book or any traditions but that they have been played around with. Had it not been for God's protection of the Qur'an from corruption and substitution then talking about it today would be like talking about the books of the other religions. God though has made sure that his light is complete and his word protected whether the unbelievers like it or not.

[22] Even the Gospels that exist today confirm this fact. In one of them appear the words: 'Do not think that I am here to nullify the words of the divine law and the prophets. I have not come to cancel but to perfect. I tell you the truth: Not one iota nor one full stop will disappear from the divine law.

[23] The Bible: Mark 9:43 and Matthew 5:27-30.

[24] Barnabas. It is well known that the Christians, for about 22 years after Christ (Peace be upon him), continued to observe all the prohibitions found in the Torah. Subsequently however, they limited them to four namely adultery, the eating of animals killed by strangling, the eating of blood, and the eating of animals slaughtered in the name of idols.

[25] The Story of Civilisation. Del Durant p.41.

[26] ibid. p.42.

[27] This is for a number of reasons, the most important of which is that animals are subject entirely to the system whereas human beings are partly responsible for administering and organising themselves.

[28] Some people have strived to prove these theories with case loads of evidence some of which raises doubts and others are dubious and obscurantist and with no proof but illusion, conjecture and

fabrication. The author has discussed the three philosophies in several books some of which are: 'A Critique of Freud', and 'Marx Defeated' and 'Comparative Economics.'

[29] What is meant here is not nature as in the natural world or surroundings but rather the intrinsic nature inside human beings known by the Arabic term *Fitrah*. (Translator's note)

[30] The Holy Qur'an: The Cow (2): 205.

[31] Ala had denied himself all the good things in life. Imam 'Ali told him: '; Do you think that Allah has made lawful for you the good things then disdains that you partake of them? You are less important to Allah than this. (Translator's note)

[32] Supplement to the Shi'a guide to Islamic law; Volume 1; Page 540. There are other benefits to marriage which have been discussed by the author in 'The Encyclopaedia of Fiqh'; Volume 62;'The Book of Marriage.

[33] The Holy Qur'an: Iron (57): 27.

[37] Shi'a Guide; Volume 15; Page 1.

[38] The Holy Qur'an: The Cow (2): 185

[39] Ghawali Al-Li'ali;Volume1;Page 381. There are many traditions referring to the desirability of a small dowry which have been dealt with by the author in *The Encyclopaedia of Fiqh;* Volume 62-68;The Book of Wedlock.

[40] The author has dealt with similar such traditions in *The Book of Fiqh, Etiquette, and Practice.* Volumes 94 -97.

[41] The author refers to practises in countries where the state does not provide any support for housing etc. In such cases the newly wed couples would continue to live with the parents. This may not be applicable in countries where state support is provided for housing. (Editor's note).

[42] The Complete Branches of Religion; Volume 5; Page 279.

[43] The Holy Qur'an: The Heights (7): 157.

[44] Shi'a Guide; volume 15; Page 1.

[45] One of the daughters of the Prophet. Fatima married 'Ali. (Translator's note)

[46] Seas of Lights: Volume 100, p 373.

[47] This is often neglected.

[48] The Holy Qur'an: The Inevitable Event (56): 37.

[49] The Holy Qur'an: Light (24): 32.

[50] *The Complete Branches of Religion*; Volume 5; Page 279.

[51] Shi'a Guide; volume 17; page 238.

[52] Seas of Lights; volume 72; page 107.

[53] Sometimes the family would give some sugar to the notary although many of them did not even accept this.

[54] Seas of Lights; Volume 2; Page 272.

[55] Seas of Lights; Volume 100; Page 372. (The Qur'an provides detailed injunctions regarding those blood relations and other persons that a person may not marry. However in Islam it is permissible for a person to marry his or her cousin as was customary in Western societies until not so very long ago.(Translator's note)).

[56] The following items are incumbent upon her religiously:
1. Undertaking the Hajj pilgrimage.
2. Learning the laws of the religion.
3. Maintaining the bond of kinship for example in visiting the parents.
4. All matters pertaining to preserving one's self and one's religion.

[57] Seas of Lights; Volume 10; Page 227.

[58] The Holy Qur'an: The Cow (2): 228.

[59] The Holy Qur'an: The Cow (2): 187.

[60] The Holy Qur'an: The Cow (2): 228.

[61] Al-Fiqh series, 'Al-Bay'a', Volumes 111-115.

[62] The Holy Qur'an: The Prohibition (66): 6.

[63] The author has dealt with the times recommended and discouraged for intercourse in The Encyclopaedia of Fiqh; The Book of Wedlock; Volume 62; Pages 112-130. Likewise in the Book of Etiquette and Practices.

[64] Psychological studies have shown that the child who is fed at the breast of his/her mother is usually less susceptible to psychological problems. The sense of security, warmth and affection which the baby feels at the mother's breast increase his/her attachment to her in the future. Also, as doctors would confirm, all attempts to find a synthetic substitute to mother's milk have failed. Mother's milk provides the complete requirements for the health of the infant and its physical and mental growth. (Our children, their growth, nutrition and their problems. 'Ali Hasan. p.70.). Also among the benefits of breastfeeding for the mother is the fact that it lessens the risk of her contracting breast cancer and helps to return the womb to its natural

state and also works to dispel spots and blemishes from the face of the mother.

[65] Shi'a Guide; Volume 3; Page 331.

[66] The Holy Qur'an: The Prohibition (66): 6.

[67] The Holy Qur'an: Women (4): 1.

[68] Seas of Lights; Volume 74; Page 94.

[69] Seas of Lights; Volume 74; Page 111.

[70] Seas of Lights; Volume 74; Page 114.

[71] Seas of Lights; Volume 74; Page 100.

[72] There are many traditions which condemn the envy and jealousy of women. These include the sayings of Imam 'Ali: *'The jealousy of a man is faith but the jealousy of a woman is enmity'* (*The Pearls of Wisdom*)., also ' *The jealousy of a woman amounts to disbelief but the jealousy of a man is faith'*(*The Summit of Eloquence*: Article 124). From the sayings of Imam Al-Baqir: ' *The jealousy of women is envy, which is the root of unbelief. Women if they are jealous become angry and if they become angry they fall into disbelief except those who are true Muslims.*(*The Complete Branches of Religion*; Volume 5; Page 505).

[73] The Holy Qur'an: The Cow (2): 229.

[74] The Holy Qur'an: The Night Journey (17): 27. The author has discussed the meaning of this verse in the sixty-second volume of *The Encyclopaedia of Fiqh*; Page 341.

[75] *The Complete Branches of Religion*; Volume 6; Page 460.

[76] See *The Encyclopaedia of Fiqh*; Volumes 76-77.

[77] Seas of Lights; Volume 72; Page 66.

[77] The Holy Qur'an: Livestock (6): 36.

[78] Grand Ayatollah Mirza Mehdi Shirazi.

[79] For example, the price of meat has risen to 48,000 times its original value, milk 75 times its value, and wheat 10,000 times its original value.

[80] The Holy Qur'an: Women (4): 35.

[81] The instance of divorce in the Islamic world has shown an unprecedented rise. In Kuwait there is one divorce for every three marriages, 29% of which take place within the first year of marriage, and 67% take place within the first five years of marriage. In Egypt there are 4 million divorced women, .The rate of divorce has risen in recent years to 25%, and the rate of cancelled engagements has risen to 15% while the rate of marriage has fallen to 20%.

[82] Supplement to Shi'a Guide; Volume 3; Page 2.

[83] Shi'a Guide; Volume 15; Page 267.

[84] Shi'a Guide; Volume 15; Page 267.

[86] The Holy Qur'an: Women(4):128.

[87] The Holy Qur'an: The Winnowing Winds (51): 49.

[88] Extracts from The Tawhid of Al-Mafdal Ibn 'Amr Al-Ga'fiyy.

[89] Seas of Lights; Volume 6; Page 98.

[90] In Egypt for example there are 3.8 million unmarried women over the age of thirty. See issue 1149 of Al-Mujtama' (Society) periodical.

[91] Studies show that 70% of the worlds poorest are women. See issue 60 of Al-Khairiyya (Charitable) periodical.

[92] Shi'a Guide; Volume 17: Page 382.

[93] The Complete Branches of Religion; Volume 5: Page 279.

[94] Shi'a Guide; Volume 13; Page 368.

[95] Seas of Lights; Volume 59; Page 283.

[96] Supplement to Shi'a Guide; Volume 14; Page 152.

[97] Ship of the Seas; Volume 1; Page 561.

[98] As in the Umayyad, 'Abbasid, or Ottoman states.

[99] There are two theories regarding childbirth:

The first is the Malthusian theory of Thomas Robert Malthus which stresses the non-correlation between demographic size and availability of economic resources since the demographic increase is subject to technology whilst economic resources are subject to arithmetic therefore equilibrium cannot be attained except through birth control. In the aftermath of the industrial revolution, Classicists promoted this theory to justify the poor distribution of incomes. In the post second world war period, certain rulers latched on to this theory to excuse the poverty, unemployment and backwardness that prevailed in their countries.

The second theory is growth theory supported by the majority of economists. It says that human behaviour depends upon the social environment and other social factors like values and traditions, and upon the extent to which Nature can be controlled, and upon the advancement of modes of production, and upon the nature of the prevailing economic system. These factors interact to influence human demographic behaviour. In other words, the absence of equilibrium between demographic growth and the nature of the economic and social system inhibits growth and prosperity. This theory believes that the best way to cure population growth is economic growth and advancement and social justice, the people not being responsible for their poverty but rather the state being responsible due to poor distribution of wealth, the failure of growth and the prevalence of unemployment due to laws which inhibit freedoms.

The Malthusian theory did not meet with any success and its overwhelming failure was proven in the countries of Europe. Hence voices have been raised in the West in criticism of the concept of birth control. Scholars say that people spontaneously are inclined to keep their numbers to reasonable levels when the standard of living rises and the economic and cultural way of life changes. The voices of criticism among Western scholars and intellectuals convinced the powers that be to bring in laws to increase reproduction rates. It may be wondered what the hidden factors were which motivated certain regimes to adopt birth control. In answer we would say that these regimes are of two types; local and Western. Local regimes have an interest in birth control as they lay the responsibility for backwardness at the door of the people and cover up their own failure to deliver economic and social growth and draw a veil over their own liabilities from bureaucracy through to corruption which contribute to the inefficacy of the growth cycle. Western regimes have an interest in birth control in the third world making them the big players on the world stage and diminishing the dependence of the third world on warranted international assistance and loans and preventing a flood of population from the third world into their countries. In addition to these factors, the application of the theory of growth in the third world means delving into three areas that the Western states would rather not delve; a).The lessening of consumption in the West, b).Third world debt, c). Transfer of technology from advanced nations to other nations. [Adapted from article called 'Two Schools of Thought in Dealing with the Population Problem' by Fahmy Haueidi].

[100] The German government spends millions yearly to encourage childrearing. Scholars believe that women only become fully matured after one or two childbirths and that many women who have not given birth are not as well balanced as mothers. This in addition to the fact that they become more nervous than the mothers. The well-known French physician Petard says: Frankly a woman will not achieve good health unless she becomes a mother.

[101] To realise the extent of Western fears about the dwindling of their populations it is enough to monitor newspapers concerned with social affairs and attend important conferences on demography in Europe. In 1988 the Danish press announced that the Danish government had imported 1000 Filipino girls for purposes of childrearing on the premise that Filipino girls are more inclined towards love, procreation and children.

[102] The Islamic world covers approximately 30% of the earth's surface amounting to 32.7 million square kilometres that equals 3.5 times the area of the United States and China.

[103] Certain people may cling to birth control for the following reasons: a). The parents may be incapable of bringing up their children. b). The 'happy life' may be one with few children and dependants. The answer to the first is that the history of Islam from the flight of the prophet until now confirms that the parents have the capacity to bring up their children and indeed upbringing is not confined to the parents alone but the whole of society takes part in it. In answer to the second, the truth is quite the opposite - the preferable life comes from having many children because life progresses through co-operation and the many necessitate more co-operation in quality and quantity.

[104] The arable land of the Sudan comes to about 300 million acres (about1200 million square kilometres) of which only 30 million acres is currently cultivated.

[105] Shi'a Guide; Volume 17: Page 328.

[106] The Complete Branches of Religion; Volume 5: Page 279.

[108] The Holy Qur'an: The Star (53): 39-40.

[109] The Diwan of Imam 'Ali.

[110] Ship of the Seas; Volume 1; Page 561.

[111] The Holy Qur'an: The Night Journey (17): 31.

[112] The Holy Qur'an: Light (24): 32.

[113] Seas of Lights; Volume 72; Page 36.

[114] In Egypt for example there are 15 million young men and women of marriageable age who are not yet married. (*Al-Mujtam'a* magazine; Issue 1149).

[115] The Holy Qur'an: Woman (4): 9.

[116] *Nahj Al-Fasaha*: Page 51

[117] Seas of Lights; Volume 33; Page 374.

[118] The Holy Qur'an: The Table Spread (5): 2.

[119] Seas of Lights; Volume 19; Page 218.

[120] The Holy Qur'an: The House of 'Emran (3): 159.

[121] The Holy Qur'an: Consultation (42): 38.

[122] The Holy Qur'an: The Cow (2): 233. The author has dealt with counsel in the book 'Counsel in Islam'. The author's son Ayatollah Murtadha Shirazi discusses it and its doctrinal and legal evidences in detail in his valuable book Counsel of Jurists.

[123] See Shi'a Guide; Volume 12; Page 129.

[124] Seas of Lights; Volume 105; Page 168.

[125] The Holy Qur'an: Public Estates (8): 24.

[126] The Holy Qur'an: (the letters) T.H. (20): 124.

[127] This refers to the welfare system devised and implemented by the Messenger of Allah, Muhammad, 14 centuries ago. (Editor's note)

[128] The Holy Qur'an: The Groups (39): 9.

[129] The Holy Qur'an: The House of 'Emran (3): 118.

[130] The Holy Qur'an: The House of 'Emran (3): 159.

[131] The Holy Qur'an: Banishment (59): 7.

[132] Seas of Lights; Volume 52; Page 312.

[133] The Holy Qur'an: (the letters) T.H. (20): 124.

[134] The Holy Qur'an: Public Estates (8): 25.

[135] The Holy Qur'an: Banishment (59):19.

[136] As an example, Issue 1364 of the Iraqi magazine 'Alef Ba' mentioned that Iraq was home to 32,000,400 date palms in the year 1952, 13 million of which were in Basra and giving 650 types of date. This number fell to 2,997,600 date palms in 1989. In recent years it has dwindled to the smallest number possible.

[137] The volume of military expenditure for the Gulf States in 1993 reached 60 billion dollars.

[138] Statistics show that loans against the Arab States including the Gulf States to the end of 1993 reached 194 billion dollars the interest upon which loans reached 18 billion dollars yearly.

The Author

Ayatollah al-Udhma Imam Muhammad Shirazi is the Religious Authority, or *Marje'*, to millions of Muslims around the globe. A charismatic leader who is known for his high moral values, modesty and spirituality, Imam Shirazi is a mentor and a source of aspiration to Muslims; and the means of access to authentic knowledge and teachings of Islam. He has tirelessly devoted himself, and his life, to the affairs of Muslims in particular, and to that of mankind in general. He has made extensive contributions in various fields of learning ranging from Jurisprudence and Theology to Politics, Economics, Law, Sociology and Human Rights.

Muhammad Shirazi was born in the holy city of Najaf, Iraq, in 1347 AH (Muslim calendar), 1927 AD. He settled in the holy city of Karbala, Iraq, at the age of nine, alongside his father. After primary education, the young Shirazi continued his studies in different branches of learning under his father's guidance as well as those of various other eminent scholars and specialists. In the course of his training he showed a remarkable talent and appetite for learning as well as a tireless commitment to his work and the cause he believed in. His extraordinary ability, and effort, earned him the recognition, by his father and other *Marje's* and scholars, of being a *Mujtahid*; a qualified religious scholar in the sciences of Islamic jurisprudence and law. He was subsequently able to assume the office of the Marje' at the early age of 33 in 1960. His followers are found in many countries around the globe.

Imam Shirazi is distinguished for his intellectual ability and holistic vision. He has written various specialized studies that are considered to be among the most important references in the Islamic sciences of beliefs or doctrine, ethics, politics, economics, sociology, law, human rights, etc. He has enriched the world with his staggering contribution of more than 1000 books, treatise and studies on various branches of learning. His works range from simple introductory books for the young generations to literary and scientific masterpieces. Deeply rooted in the holy Qur'an and the Teachings of the Prophet of Islam, his vision and theories cover areas such as Politics, Economics, Government, Management, Sociology, Theology, Philosophy, History and Islamic Law. His work on Islamic Jurisprudence (*al-Fiqh* series) for example constitutes 150 volumes, which run into more than 70,000 pages. Through his original thoughts and ideas he has championed the causes of issues such as the family, human right, freedom of expression, political pluralism, non-violence, and Shura or consultative system of leadership.

Imam Shirazi believes in the fundamental and elementary nature of freedom in mankind. He calls for freedom of expression, political plurality, debate and discussion, tolerance and forgiveness. He strongly believes in the consultative system of leadership and calls for the establishment of the leadership council of religious authorities. He calls for the establishment of the universal Islamic government to encompass all the Muslim countries. These and other ideas are discussed in detail in his books.

o-o-o-o-O-o-o-o-o

Official website of Ayatollah al-Udhma Imam Muhammad Shirazi: **www.shirazi.org.uk**

Other Publications by *fountain books*

1. Aspects of the Political Theory pf Imam Muhammad Shirazi

Muhammad Ayyub is a well-known Islamist political activist within the Iraqi circle who has established a long history of political struggle behind him. He was attracted by the views of the Imam Muhammad Shirazi in the fields of social and political sciences. This prompted the author to write this book to introduce the reader to these views that have remained relatively unknown to the Muslim activists and reformists. It covers such aspects on politics as freedom of expression, party-political pluralism and organisation, social justice, peace and non-violence, human rights, consultation system of government, etc.

2. Islamic System of Government

In this introductory book the author outlines the basic principles of government based on the teachings of Islam. The author begins with the aim and objectives of the government according to Islam and the extent of its authority. He then addresses, from the Islamic viewpoint, the significance and fundamental nature of such issues as consultative system of government, judicial system, freedoms, party political pluralism, social justice, human rights, foreign policy, etc. The author also outlines the policies of a government on issues such as education, welfare, health, crime, services, etc. as well as such matter as the government's income.

3. If Islam Were To Be Established

This book can serve as the Muslim's guide to the Islamic government. If an Islamist opposition group has a plan for an Islamic government, this book would help to check various aspects of the plan. In the absence of such a plan, this book would present one. To the non-Muslims, the book presents a glimpse of a typical Islamic system of government. The book would also serve as a yardstick for anyone to check the practices of any government that claims to have implemented an Islamic system of government.

Available form:

www.ebooks.com and
Alif International, 109 Kings Avenue, Watford, Herts. WD1 7SB, UK. Telephone: + 44 1923 240 844, Fax: +44 1923 237 722